CROSSWORDS

CROSSWORDS

SIRIUS

SIRIUS

This edition published in 2022 by Sirius Publishing, a division of
Arcturus Publishing Limited,
26/27 Bickels Yard, 151–153 Bermondsey Street,
London SE1 3HA

ISBN: 978-1-3988-2509-3
AD010785US

Printed in China

1

Across

1 Mahmoud ____, president of Palestine after Yasser Arafat
6 Amniotic ____
9 Guitarist Santana
11 Australian non-flyer
12 Tenant farmer
14 Fourth mo.
15 Abbr. after a name
16 Genetic factor, initially
17 City vehicle
18 Certain tree, before or after a fire
19 Marathoner, wrestler or golfer
21 "Wheel of Fortune" request: 2 wds.
22 Keats works
23 Break down, rot
26 Gravitate (toward)
27 ____ Grove Village, Ill.
28 Bug part
30 Ability to read minds, initially
33 1996 Olympics host nation, in short
34 "____ a date!"
35 Plato's "P"
36 Ballgoer, for short
37 Sidelong pass
39 Allen-wrench shape
40 Chauffeur's uniform
41 Turn black, maybe
42 Islamic judges

Down

1 Capital of Ghana
2 Reveals
3 Simple soup
4 Matterhorn, e.g.
5 Provider of top notes
6 Ocean floors
7 One who has lost a limb
8 Expletives
10 Effusively or insincerely emotional
13 "Go team!"
20 Peek
21 Bad marks?
23 In a concentrated manner
24 Fit to be taken in
25 Credit card material
26 Acclaimed
29 Zero, in some scores
30 Blew it
31 Lamb Chop's friend
32 Synthetic fabrics, briefly
38 "The Loco-Motion" singer, Little ____

2

Across

1 Kafka character Gregor
6 Diminish
11 Get on your feet
12 Drawing room
13 Bridget's portrayer in "Bridget Jones's Diary"
14 In what place?
15 Have a bite of
17 Complete jerk
18 Settled (a bill)
20 Birmingham's state: abbr.
22 Twofold: abbr.
23 Informal and unpretentious
26 Room in France?
28 Played on stage
30 Palin and Miles
32 Sally Field's "Norma ___"
33 Dog track org.
34 Foal's mother
35 Fond du ___, Wisc.
38 "Everybody Hates Chris" co-creator Ali
40 Age-old expression
42 "The Grapes of Wrath" actor
45 "The Three Musketeers" author
46 Gloomy, in poetry
47 Accomplishments
48 Withers

Down

1 Letters on old maps
2 Broke bread
3 Woman's silk or lace scarf
4 Three-time Masters champ
5 Summer coolers
6 In addition to: 3 wds.
7 Contemptuous outburst
8 Epithet of Athena
9 Rocky peaks
10 Chemical suffixes
16 Chinese truth
18 Peace-keeping bodies, initially
19 Down with, in Dijon: 2 wds.
21 Purebred pedigree org.
23 Unafraid
24 Kitchen gadget
25 One trip around the sun
27 Shirt size: abbr.
29 Actor Billy ___ Williams
31 Possess, in Scotland
34 Demi or Dudley
35 "Saigon" star Alan
36 Together, in music: 2 wds.
37 Originated
39 Country addresses, for short
41 Roam (about)
43 "Hawaii Five-0" actor, Daniel ___ Kim
44 MGM motto word

3

Across

1 Latin lover's word
4 KLM competitor
7 Narc's org.
10 Discontinuity
11 Place for a nap
12 Aries animal
13 Route regularly used by shipping: 2 wds.
15 Dreaded snake
16 Map abbr.
17 First word of Dante's "Inferno"
18 Anouk of "La Dolce Vita"
21 Bald ___ (symbol of America)
23 People in charge: abbr.
24 South African political party, initially
25 What Rolaids might cure
30 Patriotic society, initially
31 Chinese restaurant staple
32 Town and county in New York
35 Bank job
36 Ike's command, initially
37 Deals on Wall Street, initially
39 Born, in the society column
40 Dirigible craft
44 ___ chi (Chinese exercise)
45 Plaintive cry
46 Former football coach Parseghian
47 Alphabet chain
48 Letter afterthoughts: inits.
49 But, to Caesar

Down

1 Reno and Holder, for short
2 Fannie ___
3 Agency of the Department of Justice, initially
4 Butcher shop tool
5 First-class: hyph.
6 Mezzo-soprano singer Risë
7 Sturm und ___
8 Artist's support
9 Enough
14 Current running with the wind: 2 wds.
18 "Who ___ kidding?": 2 wds.
19 Engine part: abbr.
20 2500, to Nero
22 Female stage performer
24 Aviation prefix
26 Old form of lighting: 2 wds.
27 Three, in ancient Rome
28 Military training acad.
29 Bring home
32 Film directed by and starring Barbra Streisand
33 Mr. T and pals: hyph.
34 Auto wheel alignment: hyph.
35 Dances at Jewish weddings
38 Partiality
41 Possesses
42 Feeling of fury
43 Shock absorber

4

Across

1 Supplants
7 Old activist org.
10 Hell
11 Loafer, e.g.
12 Certain lizards
13 Pack down
14 Shocked anger
16 Aromatic root credited with medicinal properties
18 Audio-speaker stats
19 Follower of Bacchus in Ancient Greece
23 Gaucho's accessory
25 Perspire
26 Pelvic bone
28 One of a matched set
29 One ___ (singly): 3 wds.
31 Ladies of La Paz
33 After-shower application
34 Animal prized for its wool
38 "I cannot tell ___": 2 wds.
39 Long, low ridge
40 Many college grads
41 Equally hard to locate: 2 wds.

Down

1 "Pulp Fiction" star Thurman
2 E-mail ID, in short
3 South of Canada, in short
4 Forcefully reproachful protest
5 Micronesian sailboats
6 Method
7 Carpet type
8 Hemispherical roof
9 Equinox mo.
11 Theater aside: 2 wds.
15 Genetic molecules, initially
16 Karmann-___ (sports car)
17 Apple product
18 Surgery sites, for short
20 Indian tree
21 Rhine tributary
22 Sot's problem, initially
24 Garage occupant
27 Rattling rhythm instrument
30 Anklebone
31 Hacienda room
32 Three Dog Night hit "___ Coming"
33 Keyboard key
35 High ___ kite: 2 wds.
36 Midpoint: abbr.
37 Professional teacher org.

5

Across

1 Pig in ___: 2 wds.
6 Novelist Nin
11 The ___, Seuss character
12 Common tree
13 First letter, in Israel
14 Borden bovine
15 Woman's light dressing gown
17 Blood letters
18 ___ Club (discount chain)
22 Fatuous
26 Fiddle-de-___
27 The 21st, e.g.: abbr.
28 End zone scores, for short
29 Hydrocarbon ending
30 Radio hobbyist
31 Bungle, slangily: 2 wds.
33 Mtn. stat
35 "Weetzie Bat" author Francesca ___ Block
36 Water, humorously: 2 wds.
41 Fissile rock
44 Ear-related
45 One over par in golf
46 Dravidian language
47 Mgrs.' helpers
48 "Uncle Vanya" woman

Down

1 Playwright Ayckbourn
2 Warsaw native
3 Nev. neighbor
4 "High Stakes Poker" player Gabe
5 Further evidence in court: 2 wds.
6 "Float like a butterfly, sting like ___": 2 wds.
7 "Frasier" character
8 ___ nova (musical style)
9 Here, in Le Havre
10 Lord Byron's "___ Walks in Beauty"
16 Venetian boat
19 ___ Isaacs Menken, actress, painter and poet
20 Maître d's handout
21 Leak slowly
22 Dull pain
23 Navy commando
24 "You've Got a Friend ___": 2 wds.
25 Rough guess
32 Free-and-easy
34 Man's man
37 Former pashas of Algiers
38 French weapon
39 Having reclined
40 First Lady of Jazz
41 Maria Contreras-Sweet's organization, initially
42 Christmas sounds
43 Mukasey and Ashcroft, for short

6

Across

1 Airborne
6 Wine holder
9 Small lake near a larger one
11 ___ Bora (Afghan region)
12 Eastern hospice for travelers
13 24-hour bank features
14 Joint problem
15 ___ corpus (law)
17 "Four Weddings and a Funeral" actor Grant
18 Afternoon in Acapulco
19 Peach or beech
20 Catholic service book
21 Medieval stringed instrument
23 Spanish store selling wine
26 Acorn bearers
30 "Life is not ___, it is a gift": 2 wds.
31 Old-fashioned knife
32 Give the cold shoulder
34 "Zip-___-Doo-Dah"
35 Animal house?
36 Drinks with a loud sucking sound
38 Flat: hyph.
39 Double dealing
40 North Carolina capital: abbr.
41 Like "20 Questions" answers: 2 wds.

Down

1 Get off one's high horse?
2 "Last of the Breed" author Louis
3 Model railroad scale: hyph.
4 In order to get things straight: 3 wds.
5 Little piggy, maybe
6 Electorate
7 Big fleet
8 Decorative bunch of cords
10 To the ___ degree
11 McIlhenny Co. product: 2 wds.
16 Play to ___, draw: 2 wds.
20 C.E.O.'s degree, often
22 Bavarian river
23 Entruster of property
24 Princess Leia ___
25 Man in the lion's den
27 Spanish guitarist Segovia
28 Prevent from leaving: 2 wds.
29 Makes sure about: 2 wds.
33 Group of schools in one area, for short
37 Willy ___, "Exotic Zoology" author

7

Across

1 Completely clueless: 2 wds.
6 Place for a barbecue
11 Bunch
12 Be a big fan of
13 Deflect
14 Ocean ___ (big boat)
15 Working dog
17 Red dwarf, e.g.
19 Certain shark
23 Corporations: abbr.
24 Kind of fingerprint, shortly
25 "Able was I ___ I saw Elba" (famous palindrome)
26 Apropos
27 Cincy player
28 Mover's vehicle
29 Blooming necklace?
30 Downed a sub, say
31 Expend
32 Trickery
34 Took a plane
35 Rings (a bell) solemnly
37 Old photo color
40 Kind of board
43 In the midst of
44 Basin for holy water
45 Prod
46 Taste, e.g.

Down

1 "Antony and Cleopatra" prop
2 Airline no more, initially
3 Like some humor
4 Overthrow, e.g.
5 ___ nitrate, fuel additive
6 Fort's defense
7 "Farewell, François!"
8 Style, French style
9 Bad thing to raise
10 "___ the fields we go"
16 Semicircular object
17 Blast with steam
18 Lightweight helmet, in India
20 Intense aversion
21 Bump off
22 Entreaty to a subscriber
24 Pipe type
33 Squeezing (out)
34 Orchestra instrument
36 Opposite of profit
37 ___ Diego Chargers
38 Bird from Down Under
39 Legume holder
41 Au ___ (served in its own gravy)
42 Class clown, often

8

Across

1 Bagged beverage
4 "___ Wiedersehen!"
7 Shakespeare's "Much ___ About Nothing"
10 Mischievous one
11 Bearded antelope
12 Fix, as an outcome
13 Post-performance summons from an audience: 2 wds.
16 Greek vowel
17 Equipped
18 Speech sounds
21 Thornton Wilder's "___ Town"
22 Christian ___
23 Prepare for winter takeoff: hyph.
26 Sacred text
30 ___-di-dah
32 Crack
33 Piece of rock or metal from outer space
36 Microwave option
38 540 degrees over the ice
39 Responsiveness to external stimuli
43 "___ you serious?"
44 Bloodshot
45 Glasgow denial
46 ___ publica
47 Prior to, palindromically
48 Martini ingredient

Down

1 Idiosyncrasy
2 Lean meat choice
3 Deductive: 2 wds.
4 Marble material
5 Eastern Christian
6 A high old time
7 Most Meccans
8 Herb with salmon
9 Eye up and down
14 Heavy weight
15 Chocolate bean
18 Pea container
19 Cry's partner
20 Drive to distraction
24 Hammock cords
25 Enjoy oysters, say
27 Banister
28 Emulate William Hurt
29 Born, in wedding announcements
31 Firearm, slangily
33 Horse hairs
34 Rust, e.g.
35 Race, as a motor
36 Autocrat until 1917
37 In this place
40 Anger
41 Mai ___
42 Dollar rival

9

Across

1 Ingrain, as into memory
5 Consider unlikely
10 "Hurray!"
12 Of an arm bone
13 "___ Mine" (1985 sci-fi movie)
14 Member of a traveling people: var.
15 Bambi, for one
17 Approximately: 2 wds.
18 In a funk
20 "Hogwash!"
22 Two or more eras, in geologic time
23 "Good grief!"
25 Command
27 Mutual relationship
31 Dermatologist's concern
32 Canyon sound
33 Cheer
35 Bon or won follower
37 Pull behind, as a boat
38 Kind of column: hyph.
40 Legal introduction?
42 "It's been ___ pleasure": 2 wds.
44 Gibberish
47 "Saturday Night Fever" setting
48 Nonsensical
49 Cold shower?
50 Don't stet

Down

1 Check out
2 Spring Break souvenir, maybe
3 Yellow dairy product: 2 wds.
4 Batter's-box focus
5 Emulated a gopher
6 Hodgepodge
7 Erratic
8 ___ profundo
9 Check for fit: 2 wds.
11 ___ and terminer (criminal court)
16 Fancy desk
18 "Just a ___" ("hold on"): abbr.
19 "Many moons ___ …"
21 Contents of some bags
24 Drought-stricken
26 Downed
28 French 101 verb
29 "I found you!"
30 "___ what?"
33 Pikes, e.g.
34 May's predecessor
36 Brings in, like a crook
39 Small river fish
41 Bust, so to speak
43 Fortune
45 Building addition
46 Caustic soap stuff

10

Across

1 Bee product
4 Some sports cars, initially
7 Lincoln's state, for short
10 1972 treaty subj.
11 50–50, e.g.
12 It's mostly nitrogen
13 Investment option, initially
14 Kind of mark
16 "A" in the alphabet: 2 wds.
18 Family folk
19 "___ tu"
20 Head, in Rome
22 Lawful
25 "Infestation" rock group
26 "Que ___"
27 Like a nerd
29 Alvin of dance
30 Latin abbrs.
31 "Automatic for the People" band
32 Combined appliance: hyph.
37 Solar System's fourth-largest planet by diameter
38 Bigger than med.
39 Heckler's hoot
40 "Angels & Demons" author ___ Brown
41 "___ Heldenleben": R. Strauss
42 Colony crawler
43 German compass point
44 Govt. agency that has your number

Down

1 Dickensian child
2 Rock shelter at the base of a cliff
3 Treasure map phrase: 4 wds.
4 Active volcano in Sicily: abbr., 2 wds.
5 Demoiselle
6 Marine creature: 2 wds.
7 Measures of distance at sea: 2 wds.
8 Ireland, to the Irish
9 ___ Rabbit, Fox or Wolf
15 More banded
17 Wait it out: 2 wds.
20 Capote, to his friends
21 Suffix with Jacob
23 British verb ending
24 Longest river in Scotland
28 False start?
29 Passionate
32 Ladies sports org.
33 Long, long time
34 Genetic molecules, initially
35 Auspices: var.
36 Actress Sofer of soaps

11

Across

1 Near-sighted
7 Banquet
10 Eye site
11 Ltr. addenda
12 Cover for the center of a car wheel
13 Superlative suffix
14 Figures
16 From that time: 2 wds.
19 ___-mo cameras
20 Nocturnal Asian primate
22 "Raiders of the Lost Ark" producer George
26 Add color to
27 In need of scratch?
28 Betel palm
29 Congressman
30 Mouths, in zoology
32 Minor bones to pick
33 Join in: 3 wds.
37 Salt Lake City college team
38 Kay Thompson title imp
42 Café au ___
43 Renée of "The Big Parade"
44 Channel that reruns "Family Feud": inits.
45 Give out again, as cards

Down

1 Dash inits.
2 "___ rang?"
3 Gambling inits.
4 Oregon's western border: 2 wds.
5 Make ___ adventure: 2 wds.
6 Native Egyptians in the Roman period
7 Graf ___
8 Nation disbanded in 1991, briefly
9 Attention-getters
11 Eat everything in sight: 4 wds.
15 ___ Island National Monument
16 Sask. neighbor
17 Evening, in Paris
18 Alencon's department
21 Beatle Ringo
23 251 in Roman numerals
24 "Cat on ___ Tin Roof": 2 wds.
25 Dict. entries
31 "Don't shed ___": 2 wds.
33 Sofia's country: abbr.
34 Greek vowels
35 One end of a hammer head: var.
36 Shoppe sign word
39 Extreme soreness
40 Baltic or Irish
41 Elver's elder

12

Across

1 Batty
5 Permits
11 Jamaican tangelo
12 Cowboy of the South American pampas
13 Former British prime minister, Neville ___ (1869–1940)
15 Indian tongue
16 Bursts of wind
17 Water barrier
19 Condition marked by chest pain
22 Norse literary work
26 Contrast between similar things
28 Delight, slangily
29 Cash in a record store
30 Coin with 118 ridges
31 Artillery burst
35 Decrease, as popularity
39 Having all its sides of the same length
41 Powerful car engines
42 Says "When?"
43 "Any ___?"
44 Be defeated

Down

1 Water carrier
2 Eastern pooh-bah
3 Hoax, informally
4 Shyness
5 Gray, in a way
6 Above average in size
7 "Little" comic strip character
8 Wood sorrels
9 Iota
10 Princes, e.g.
14 Buckwheat pancakes
18 System of Japanese writing
19 Much spam, for short
20 Common soccer score
21 Govt. purchasing group
22 Heavenly
23 When repeated, a baby's evening meal
24 "Mad Men" protagonist Draper
25 "___ takers?"
27 Doomsday cause, maybe
30 Grief
31 Tartan pattern
32 Band with the hit "Barbie Girl"
33 Just read the post and comments, say
34 Feeling you get about someone, informally
36 Words with "I'm told" or "I thought": 2 wds.
37 Two states: abbr.
38 "Hand it over or ___!"
40 Bubblehead

13

Across

1 Candy buys
5 "Empire Falls" writer Richard
10 Burn soother
11 Less big
12 Approximate
13 It's uproariously funny
14 Production of electricity
16 Front and back, at the course
17 Predicated (on)
20 Post-op therapy
24 SALT signer, initially
25 Pre-, poetically
26 You can see right through them, briefly
29 Number in a trio
31 Brazen woman
33 Extra components: 2 wds.
38 Frugality
39 Radio tuner
40 Snares
41 Brown family member
42 Boozehound
43 Give the appearance of

Down

1 Attention getter
2 Direction at sea
3 Horse color
4 Extremely peaceful
5 Lawless one
6 Foolish
7 Feed holder
8 Caught sight of
9 Bobby of hockey fame
11 Comparison word
15 Cleanse
17 School transportation
18 Egyptian cobra
19 Bill accompanier, initially
21 ___ Royal Highness
22 "___ we alone?"
23 Certain line
27 ___ longue
28 He rides the waves
29 Cookery amt.
30 Seven daughters of Atlas in Greek myth
32 Adjusts, as an alarm clock
33 "Get out of here!"
34 Support, with "up"
35 Ingredient in paella
36 Container weight
37 Bad part of town
38 Explosive, initially

14

Across

1 Brief outline
7 "What are the ___?"
11 "The Picture of ___ Gray" (Oscar Wilde novel)
12 "___ #1!"
13 Somnambulist
15 Book part
16 Amaze
17 Where lessons take place
21 "___ Force One" (1997 Harrison Ford film)
22 Oarsmen
25 Follower of Aristotle
28 Kind of show: hyph.
29 "Down under" fowl
30 Spat out in small puffs
33 "The ___ and the Pendulum"
35 "Rules for Radicals" author Alinsky
36 Offer of reconciliation: 2 wds.
41 Former iPod model
42 One-dimensional
43 Book part
44 Funds

Down

1 "Inc." spots?
2 Campaign pro.
3 Bard's before
4 Cambodian coins
5 Accessories for vampires
6 Not justifiable
7 Barn bird
8 Metric unit of length
9 Attracted
10 All dried up
14 Like the game, to Holmes
17 Crime boss
18 Bank claim
19 Bringing to a standstill
20 "I ___ you one"
23 Icy coating
24 Soviet ballistic missile
26 Mischievous one
27 Temporary inactivity
31 2006 Olympics host
32 African antelope
33 Ceremonial splendor
34 Pelvic bones
37 "C'est la ___!"
38 Logical lead-in
39 Crow's call
40 "48 ___"

15

Across

1 Chilly
6 Female gametes
9 Christmas wish, for many
10 A thousand thou
11 Act the dictator
13 Petty officer
14 Bridge declaration
17 Certain ear parts
21 Frequently, for short
22 Indistinct
23 Movement by successive stages
26 Combined for common benefit
27 Tokyo, formerly
28 Jellied garnish
29 Raised, as steer
30 Sudden upswing
33 Male head of a family
37 Be in debt
38 Biblical mount
39 Dark time for poets
40 Prepared to propose

Down

1 Liable
2 "Law," in Spanish
3 Clothes
4 Aviation org.
5 Bears' lairs
6 Inauspicious
7 As follows: abbr.
8 Barley-based beverage
12 Cancels
14 Old man
15 Rounded thickly curled hairdos
16 Bend down
18 Thorny plant
19 Crumble to the sea, as shoreline
20 Church assembly
22 Hospital unit
24 Gleam
25 Come again
29 European capital
31 Insurer's calculation
32 Close the gap
33 "The Black Cat" writer
34 Blow away
35 ___ Poly
36 Billboard chart-topper

16

Across

1 Eruption spillage
5 East and West, in the U.S.
11 "The Wages of Fear" actor Montand
12 Cry of dismay: 2 wds.
13 Muralist José Maria ___
14 Kind of rug
15 Forbidding
17 Calendar units
19 Looped handle on an ancient vase
22 "… His wife could ___ lean": 2 wds.
23 Swindled
25 Egg: prefix
26 Cantonese dish
27 Swansea residents
30 Be ___ in the neck: 2 wds.
32 Audition tape
33 Actress Gibbs
34 Angry
36 Eur.'s largest active volcano: 2 wds.
39 Loughlin of "Full House"
42 Curved structures
43 Mirror-conscious
44 Boar's abode
45 Sidi ___, Morocco

Down

1 Fleur-de-___
2 Caesar's hello
3 Adaptable
4 Back at sea
5 Ice cream holder
6 Margaret Mitchell family
7 Pre-Christmas season
8 Red or Dead, e.g.
9 Atlantic City casino, with "The"
10 Breaking capacity, briefly
16 International charitable grp.
17 Yelp of sudden pain
18 With overhangs
20 Rio de Janeiro's ___ Mountain: 2 wds.
21 Carpenter's need: 2 wds.
24 Actress Gershon
28 Blues singer Bessie and sculptor David
29 Large social wasp
30 Big inits. in bowling
31 Pope from 1963–78: 2 wds.
35 "No problem!"
36 Blueprint
37 Prefix with angle
38 Arrhythmia detector, initially
40 ___ Tin Tin
41 Cecil Campbell, a.k.a. ___ Kamoze

17

Across

1 Chain of hills
6 Milk: prefix
11 Early year: 2 wds.
12 Southernmost city of Israel
13 Checkerberry
15 Bullfight cheer
16 Long sweeping uppercut in boxing
17 Metered vehicles
20 Jerry Lewis's telethon org.
22 Chicken ____ King: 2 wds.
23 In an overly huge way
27 Yuletide tune: 2 wds.
29 Targeted: 2 wds.
30 "How Can ____ Sure?" (hit of 1967): 2 wds.
31 Application datum letters
32 "Back in the ____"
33 Dundee denizen
36 "____ Freischütz" (Weber opera)
38 Festive
43 Whisky ____, L.A. nightclub: 3 wds.
44 Actress Massey
45 Singer Cherry, whose albums include "Buffalo Stance"
46 Track set in a table for a router: hyph.

Down

1 Aisle
2 Kamoze of reggae
3 Cave
4 Spanish felines
5 Noble, in Essen
6 Gam
7 Center for military planes
8 1963 role for Liz
9 Old Chinese money
10 "My Heart Can't Take ____ More" (1960s hit for The Supremes): 2 wds.
14 Influential Dutch artist (1606–69)
17 Hombre's home
18 "Others" in a Latin phrase
19 Soothing ointment
21 Balance sheet item
23 Big ref. works, for short
24 Ivy League team
25 Law degrees, initially
26 1914 battle line
28 Trace
32 Europe-Asia divider
33 Look over quickly
34 Cr. transaction
35 Hebrew name for Uranus
37 Send forth
39 Fifth note in a musical scale
40 Another word for the Sun
41 ____ Balls (snack cakes)
42 China's Sun ____-sen

18

Across

1 Capital of Pas-de-Calais
6 Garden squirter
10 Command to a horse: 2 wds.
11 Songbirds
12 "Great minds think ___"
13 Be in store for
14 A round of secs.
15 Aviary sound
17 1773 jetsam
18 Big blackbird
19 007, for one
20 Food scrap
21 Bundled off
23 Car for a coffin
25 In pieces
27 Possessive pronoun
30 Ram, for one
34 Common cyst of the skin
35 It's three, on some clocks
37 Actor Alastair
38 Ancient
39 Down in the dumps
40 ___ and cheese
41 Necklace parts, maybe
43 Bizarre
45 Dental work
46 "Halt!" to a salt
47 Chat
48 Shoots in the foot, e.g.

Down

1 Certain lizards
2 Repair, as a coat
3 Bring under control: 2 wds.
4 Arctic bird
5 Blueprint data
6 Hesitate to act
7 Henry Clay, for one
8 Those who travel on the piste
9 Fancy home
11 Attorney
16 Loss of ability to understand words
22 Clavell's "___-Pan"
24 Cash dispenser, initially
26 Too uptight
27 Cheesy: hyph.
28 Actress Bonham Carter
29 Ultimate object: hyph.
31 Guru's headquarters
32 Be a go-between
33 Ants
36 Absolutely perfect
42 S. ___, 40th state
44 "Uncle Tom's Cabin" girl

19

Across

1 Shampoo target
6 Gallant mount
11 Fusion
12 Enemies of the Iroquois
13 Chopper blade
14 Flowing tresses
15 Support one person against another: 2 wds.
17 In harmony: 2 wds.
18 Nearly all
21 Calcified deposit on the teeth
25 Diving bird
26 NASDAQ unit: abbr.
27 Rest time: abbr.
28 Display on a pedestal
30 Person in charge
31 Wrong step
33 Lacking a distinctive form
37 Woman in a "Paint Your Wagon" song
38 Old hat
40 "___ What You Make It" (Hannah Montana song)
41 Up ___ (trapped): 2 wds.
42 Not quite right
43 Young hog

Down

1 Genealogically-based community service organization, initially
2 Blood vessel obstruction
3 ___Vista (search engine)
4 Analyze: 2 wds.
5 Funeral heaps
6 Meeting for an exchange of ideas
7 Business person
8 Article for Mozart
9 Wide widths, initially
10 Community studies deg.
16 Gloater's phrase: 2 wds.
18 Family heads
19 No longer burning
20 Jamaican music
22 General ___'s chicken (Chinese restaurant dish)
23 "___ in apple": 2 wds.
24 Tony Dorsett, John Riggins, etc.
26 Be greater than
29 Makes fun of
30 Inhalation
32 As ___ Methuselah: 2 wds.
33 Singer Whitman
34 Stereo system: hyph.
35 Stage name of Brian Vaughn Bradley, Jr.
36 "To ___ World in a Grain of Sand" (William Blake, "Auguries of Innocence"): 2 wds.
37 Italian note
39 Police rank, briefly

20

Across

1 "Sea of Trees" director Gus Van ___
5 Medicinal shrub
11 Cream ingredient
12 Consume more than
13 Filmmaker Wertmüller
14 Conundrum
15 Mentalist's claim, shortly
16 ___'acte (intermission)
17 Former East German secret police
19 Poker concession: 2 wds.
23 E.R. personnel
24 Boo-boo
25 Away from port
27 Charged particles
28 Equally
30 Ron of the 1970s–80s Dodgers
31 Floating log competition
32 Cable channel that shows Senate hearings: hyph.
35 Mazda sub-compact vehicle: hyph.
37 52, in Ancient Rome
38 Cold War adjective
41 Showed up
42 Bank customer's ID: abbr., 2 wds.
43 Footnote abbr.: 2 wds.
44 Meryl of "Julie & Julia"
45 Back muscles, to a personal trainer

Down

1 Corporate department
2 Most sought-after group: hyph.
3 One of a kind
4 Drink in the afternoon
5 "Burn After Reading" director
6 Pop's sister
7 Prepares Chinese vegetables: 2 wds.
8 Line part: abbr.
9 "___ a Rock" (Simon & Garfunkel hit): 2 wds.
10 ___ glance (quickly): 2 wds.
16 Cologne cooler
18 Injury caused by an asp, e.g.
20 Montana's state motto that means "gold and silver" in Spanish: 3 wds.
21 Ban-___ (brand of synthetic yarn)
22 Physicians: abbr.
25 Rhine feeder
26 Classic candy, ___ Poke
29 Epoch preceding the Oligocene
30 "Bad Moon Rising" band, briefly
33 Get in the cross hairs: 2 wds.
34 ___ Arden Oplev, director of "Dead Man Down"
36 At the apex of
38 Carrier to Sweden, initially
39 Columbus Day mo.
40 DVD player's predecessor
41 Animation collectible

21

Across

1 Drugs in "Brave New World"
6 Special effects used in "Avatar," e.g.
9 Roof growth in winter
11 Bolted
12 Bath powder
13 BFGoodrich product
14 Herb of the marjoram genus
16 Aquatic bloodsucker
18 Insect's feeler
19 Loafer, e.g.: hyph.
23 Convex molding
25 Night noise
26 Green film on copper
28 Assertively dynamic: hyph.
29 Argumentative, pugnacious
31 Until now
34 ___ d'amore
35 "1984" author
39 Motley
40 Smooth-textured smoked sausage
41 Drivers' licenses, at times
42 Sharp, narrow ridge found in rugged mountains

Down

1 Brood
2 Mozart's "L'___ del Cairo"
3 Dot follower, in some e-mail addresses
4 Highly trained or skilled
5 Drink out loud
6 Front of the lower jaw
7 Know-it-all
8 Any thing
10 Kuwait rulers
11 Stamina: 2 wds.
15 Hair goops
16 Magma, after surfacing
17 All the time: 2 wds.
18 "___ Goes the Weasel"
20 Boring sort
21 Bacchanal
22 Introduction to Latin?
24 "___ upon a time…"
27 Bow and ___
30 Central, open areas
31 Arizona tribe
32 In the same place, in a bibliog.
33 Temperature testers, maybe
36 Direction away from WSW
37 Blotto
38 Arlington owner

22

Across

1 Bros, e.g.
5 Musically connected
11 Tech. product reviews
12 Real: 2 wds.
13 That's ___ concern: 2 wds.
14 Book after Nehemiah
15 Look back regretfully on
16 Difficult obligation
17 Furnish with a fund
19 Blot out
23 Bad thing to raise
24 Ten-cent coins
25 In-basket stamp: abbr.
27 ___ jockey
28 Opposing parties
30 "___ appetit!"
31 Fire starter
32 Days ___: 2 wds.
35 Dance and drama, for example
37 River to the Rhine
38 Stand-up comedian Carrington
41 Height, in combination
42 Actress Sissy of "Carrie"
43 One-named singer for the 1960s Velvet Underground
44 Tampa neighbor, briefly: 2 wds.
45 What Ritalin treats, for short

Down

1 Make a goal
2 Just for laughs: 2 wds.
3 Pope from 575–79: 2 wds.
4 Pou ___, basis of operation
5 Claim
6 Followed
7 Removes: 3 wds.
8 Cigar stuff
9 Literary inits.
10 Donne's "done"
16 Have debts
18 Authoritative order
20 Simple organic compound: 2 wds.
21 French possessive
22 PC bailout button
25 W.W. II fighter pilots' gp.
26 Certain photo order: abbr.
29 Highway
30 Actress Derek and singer Diddley
33 Tough, durable wood
34 Dickens's Edwin
36 Kid
38 Web letters in an orange button
39 Make a decision
40 Touch lightly on the water
41 Gasteyer of "Mean Girls"

23

Across

1 Talk, talk, talk
4 Campaigned for office
7 Calif., Fla., Ill., etc.
8 "___ on a Grecian Urn"
9 Half a sawbuck
12 "___ be seeing you"
13 Russian empress: var.
15 Musical endings
17 City near the mouth of the River Douro
18 Grand story
19 Consider
20 TV dramas, generally
24 ___ Lanka (Asian island nation)
25 China, Japan, et al.: 2 wds.
27 Consumes
29 Buccaneer's blade
32 ___ hygiene
34 Spin like ___: 2 wds.
35 Back tooth
37 Coward's lack, figuratively
38 Issue, as from a source
40 "A Chorus Line" number
41 Family man
42 Draper of "Mad Men"
43 "Waking ___ Devine" (1998 film)
44 Boozer
45 Babe's home

Down

1 Health bar offerings
2 Going downhill?
3 Dish of apples, walnuts, celery, etc.: 2 wds.
4 Enormous birds of myth
5 Timberjack's tool
6 One of the tides
9 Places where dalmatians are mascots: 2 wds.
10 "State" or "national" starter
11 Gore-ista Wolf
14 Bacillus shape
16 "Bamboo curtain" locale
21 Leap across a gap, electrically
22 Romanian monetary unit
23 Convened
26 High-five, e.g.
27 ___ in on (got closer)
28 Bakery attraction
30 Italian poem
31 Express
33 Ofc. computer link
36 X-ray units
37 Delighted
39 "Not a moment ___ soon!"

24

Across

1 Track circuit
4 Port city of southern Alabama
10 Peace Nobelist Wiesel
12 Encroachment
13 Novelist Morrison
14 Actions
15 Unexcitable
17 Motown's original name
19 French seasoning
22 Refined
24 Microsoft anti-infringement system, initially
25 Prefix with skeleton
26 100 bani in Romania
27 Frozen water in Germany
28 N.Y. engineering sch.
29 Most moist
31 Country west of Alg.
32 Like ___ (probably): 2 wds.
33 City district associated with musicians, ___ Alley: 2 wds.
36 Already recorded: 2 wds.
41 Place for a béret
42 Warming device
43 Spoke up
44 Highly-prized game fish
45 French possessive

Down

1 Answer to "Shall we?"
2 Frequently: 2 wds.
3 Black grape variety
4 From Kuwait or Iran, e.g.: 2 wds.
5 Yoko of "Dear Yoko"
6 Man's nickname
7 Tiny particle
8 Jet effect
9 Bradley and Meese
11 Southernmost city of Israel
16 Mrs. Marcos
18 College graduates
19 Plants with colorful, fragrant flowers
20 Sponsorship: var.
21 Survive
22 Disease cause
23 Large international show
30 French bridges
34 Play to ___, draw: 2 wds.
35 Beatty and Flanders
36 Electrical unit
37 Prof's org.
38 Driveway surface
39 N.L. East city
40 Louvre Pyramid architect

25

Across

1 Medicinal plant
6 "___ cap fits, wear it": 2 wds.
11 Sing like Bing
12 Big name in Scotch whisky
13 Gymnastics apparatus
14 Blue-pencils
15 Be absent from
17 Real: Ger.
18 1950s talk-show pioneer
20 Wrap in waxed cloth
22 Engine part: abbr.
23 Gyrates
26 Timepiece that sounds like a bird: 2 wds.
28 Followers of a Chinese philosophy
29 Actress Myrna
30 1997 Peter Fonda role
31 Between assignments
32 "I get it," jokily: 2 wds.
34 Balance
36 Indian yogurt dish
38 "Delta of Venus" author ___ Nin
41 Reply to a playground insult: 2 wds.
42 Convinces
43 Simple question type: 2 wds.
44 Canned meat rival of Spam

Down

1 Coll., e.g.
2 Canyon or ranch ending
3 Famed proponent of nuclear disarmament: 2 wds.
4 Adamant refusal: 2 wds.
5 Hydrocarbon suffixes
6 Chemical ending
7 Kind of case
8 Hackneyed story: hyph., 2 wds.
9 "He that ___ a beard is more than a youth" (Shakespeare)
10 At first, once
16 Two-wheeled vehicle
18 Ancient Briton
19 The rain in Spain
21 List enders, briefly
23 Red, red flower
24 Biol. branch
25 ___ Terrier
27 Two million pounds
31 Tennis player John
32 "Knowledge can split ___ of light" (Dickens): 2 wds.
33 Curved part of a draft horse's collar
35 Toward sunrise
37 From ___ Z: 2 wds.
39 ___ de France
40 Retired flier's letters

26

Across

1 Shot a certain spray at
6 Recipe amts.
11 Make ___ of (highlight): 2 wds.
12 Capital of Yemen
13 Met. Opera house mural painter: 2 wds.
15 Beer brand, initially
16 Propel, in a way
17 Close one
18 Spanish hoop
19 Print anew
21 Friendly dogs, for short
23 "Crossfire" network
24 Like some Fr. nouns
26 Ambience
29 Moo goo ___ pan
31 Florida city, informally
33 Restaurant seater
37 Day of rest and worship: abbr.
38 Blood-group letters
39 Crafty
40 Shogun's capital
41 Showing poise and confidence in one's own worth: hyph.
44 "___ as the eye can see": 2 wds.
45 "You ___ a favor": 2 wds.
46 Joins (up with)
47 Feet, according to Ovid

Down

1 Warm-blooded creature
2 Meth is one of them
3 Nicaragua money
4 And more, for short
5 Drapes, pictures, etc.
6 Catherine the Great, e.g.
7 Lunch holder, maybe
8 Breaks suddenly
9 Pacific island group
10 French explorer La ___
14 "___ Dies" William Byrd motet
20 Rebuff
22 Army N.C.O.
25 Vegas venue, ___ Palace
27 Color that's like that of a flower: 2 wds.
28 Campus life
30 Archipelago units: abbr.
32 Dwellings
33 Attacks vigorously: 2 wds.
34 Corpulent
35 Musical syllable system: hyph.
36 Online administrator, briefly: 2 wds.
42 Relatives, slangily
43 "Assault on Wall Street" director Boll

27

Across

1 Place to unwind
4 Flock sound
7 Enormous
10 Carbon dating estimate
11 ___ sprouts
13 Bone-knitting aid: 2 wds.
15 Salad, often
16 Mythical monster
17 Humorist
20 Barely manages, with "out"
23 Bends
26 Mai ___ (cocktail)
27 Woody Herman or Woody Allen, e.g.
29 Eminem's genre
30 County in southeastern England
31 Knucklehead
33 Baltic or Aegean
34 "Can't Help Lovin' ___ Man" (Ella Fitzgerald)
36 Arrived
40 Damage from ordinary use: 3 wds.
44 In transit, in France: 2 wds.
45 Genetic matter, briefly
46 Ottoman governor
47 Lord's Prayer pronoun
48 "Certainly!"

Down

1 Lights-out signal at camp
2 Large tangelo
3 Bracelet piece
4 Cave dweller
5 Beer variety
6 1960s hairdo
7 Formal dinner wear: 2 wds.
8 Possibilities
9 Hood's gun, shortly
12 Big field
14 Ratty place
18 Allies' foe
19 Biological classification
21 "Piece of cake!"
22 Command to a dog
23 Imperfection
24 Expert in stone engraving
25 All dried up
27 PC component
28 Plot of land
32 Starch source
35 Drawn tight
37 Ethereal
38 Lion's hair
39 Historic spans
40 Spider's home
41 Helm heading, initially
42 Imprecise ordinal
43 Susan of "The Partridge Family"

28

Across

1 "Let's play ___": 2 wds.
6 Michelangelo masterpiece
11 Symbol of slowness
12 Textile trademark
13 Yemen's capital
14 Indian yogurt dish
15 California's Fort ___
16 Elvis Presley's "___ Lost You"
18 Group of whales
19 Less dirty
21 String between L and P
22 Sleuth: abbr.
23 Waters, in Paris
24 Never-ending
27 This and that
28 Indian P.M., 1991–6
29 Card needed for blackjack
30 Dead body of an animal
34 "Quiet down!" sounds
35 "The Ice Storm" director Lee
36 Hosp. aide
37 Assumed name
39 "Dallas" matriarch Miss ___
41 Minimal
42 Spanish seven
43 Ancient city in Egypt
44 Leo of "You Make Me Feel Like Dancing"

Down

1 Org.
2 Knot
3 "Biography" network: 3 wds.
4 Italian pronoun
5 Hendrix and May
6 Kitchen implement
7 Money for later years, initially
8 Mysteries
9 Bacterial disease
10 Cottonwood trees
17 Person who has served in the military
20 Wife of Esau
23 Anti-discrimination group, initially
24 Spiral cavity of the ear
25 Eastern Mediterranean summer wind
26 Generosity in bestowing gifts
27 Igneous rock
30 Throws, as a stone
31 Back street
32 Malice
33 Derisive look
38 Faulkner's "___ Lay Dying": 2 wds.
40 ___ Fail, Irish coronation stone

29

Across

1 Enticement
5 Green, white and herbal tea company
11 Dead against
12 Bewitch
13 Dance move
14 Commercial cost, briefly: 2 wds.
15 Blind comparisons of flavors: 2 wds.
17 More than chubby
18 Astute
21 Nothing at all, slangily
25 Butter portion
26 Monthly pub.
27 Ways to go?: abbr.
29 Indian gentlemen
32 Opera singer Ezio
34 Bargain shrewdly: 2 wds.
39 Damage the purity or appearance of
40 Sea east of the Caspian
41 Click beetle
42 Vicious and Caesar
43 XC in Roman numerals
44 Manuscript encl.

Down

1 Fiber for ropes
2 Architectural pier
3 Suffix with webs or works
4 Move silently
5 In a chair
6 Peruvian peaks
7 Captain in a Jack London book
8 Last of a Latin trio
9 Specks
10 "The best things in life ___ free"
16 "Stuart Little" author's initials
18 Cal. quarter
19 Beret or bonnet
20 Numbered hwy.
22 Who or where follower: 2 wds.
23 Soupçon
24 Holder and RFK, for short
28 Fairy tale figure
29 Contemptuous
30 Antiviral drug, initially
31 Plague
33 Archipelago member
34 Prefix with port
35 End ___ era: 2 wds.
36 What the "fat lady" sings
37 Pops
38 "Where ___ could it be?"
39 Wild animal's hidden home

30

Across

1 18-wheelers
6 Did some cobbling
11 Best guests: hyph.
12 Figurative use of a word
13 Beta's follower
14 Have dinner at home: 2 wds.
15 Drug used before surgery
17 Continental coin
18 Frozen spike
22 Crucifix
26 NBC morning show
27 Around
28 Ersatz bed, to Brits
29 Monkey bread tree
30 Black mark or stain
32 In a cheerful way
38 Like smokestacks
39 Ape in "The Jungle Book"
40 ___ Novo (Benin's capital)
41 Philadelphia's state, briefly
42 Black ___ (winterberry)
43 "Ragged Dick" author

Down

1 Detailed account
2 Brio
3 Charades, essentially
4 Doctrines
5 Majestic
6 Have the helm
7 Handel's "Messiah," for one
8 Author of "Matelot" (1893)
9 Cast-of-thousands movie
10 Hibernation site
16 Gradation of color
18 "___ be hilarious!"
19 Lovey-dovey sound
20 Drivers' licenses, passports, etc.
21 Car stereo input
23 Heavenly sphere
24 Goose, in Galicia
25 Apply lightly
27 Tree with heart-shaped leaves
29 Commuting option
31 City Hall leader
32 Betting group
33 British House denizen
34 Christmas carol
35 Chinese tree cultivated for its oil
36 Actor's words
37 365 days, usually
38 Bath bath

31

Across

1 "Desert Island Discs" producer
4 Easy as pie
10 Butler, for Gable
12 Like a fact
13 Seed appendage
14 Flinches, perhaps
15 Big red deer
17 Jay and Audubon
19 Physique, informally
22 Length of film made for movies
24 "I see!"
25 Cummerbund cousin
26 "The West Wing" network
27 "___-ching!"
28 Waiting period, seemingly
29 Coarse-haired sheep of central Asia
31 Put in rollers, as hair
32 "Call it ___" (1934 Henry Roth novel)
33 Dead: 2 wds.
36 Striking or memorable phrase
41 "Hey, what's the big ___?"
42 Above and beyond the call of duty
43 Benjamin Disraeli, e.g.
44 Rush violently
45 Albanian coin

Down

1 Superb
2 Cold, violently gusty Adriatic wind
3 Expensive nightclub, informally: 2 wds.
4 Scale that works by Hooke's Law: 2 wds.
5 Dudgeon
6 Extinct bird
7 Pipe material, for short
8 Authorize
9 Lt.'s inferior
11 "Four Quartets" poet
16 Expresses gratitude
18 Hush-hush
19 Reverse one's previous opinion
20 Honolulu's island
21 Indian dish made with stewed legumes: var.
22 Adversaries
23 A musette pipe is a small one
30 Home to a condor
34 Dry
35 Speak
36 "Quiet!"
37 Monetary unit of Romania
38 Bobby of the Bruins
39 Figured out
40 Have what's "going around"

32

Across

1 Emmy-winning Thompson
5 Minor tiff
11 Cold treats
12 Meteor indentation
13 Plant-eating insect
15 "Like, that's so obvious!": 2 wds.
16 Barrels for storing liquids
17 Inlets
19 Physicist Angström
22 Untouchables, et al.: hyph.
26 Republic in West Africa, capital Freetown
28 iPhone buys
29 Cash register key: 2 wds.
30 Formal agreement
31 Virtual meeting of a sort
35 Nicholson Baker story: 3 wds.
39 Gaze that indicates no interest: 2 wds.
41 Ab ___ (from the beginning)
42 Medical suffix
43 Mislaying
44 Deeply engrossed

Down

1 Capricorn, for one
2 Prefix with bat or phobia
3 No longer living
4 They make you feel confident
5 PTA concern
6 Gators' relatives
7 ___ Nui (Easter Island)
8 Biol. energy sources
9 Secret look
10 Bungles
14 Bake, as eggs
18 Yoga posture
19 Cool ___ cucumber: 2 wds.
20 Chill
21 Passbook abbr.
22 Person who makes a will
23 Extinct flightless bird
24 Certain photo order: abbr.
25 Born, in French
27 Point
30 Corral: 2 wds.
31 Agatha Christie's "___ Under the Sun"
32 "Hawaii Five-O" nickname
33 Galatea's love in Greek myth
34 Jacques of "Mon Oncle"
36 Government org. "launched" in 1958
37 Faucet annoyance
38 Superlative suffix
40 Dress up, with "out"

33

Across

1 "It is" in France
5 Insect stages
10 End of ___: 2 wds.
12 Heart chambers
13 Reigns over
14 Brings up
15 Kennel sound
16 Michigan's ___ Canals
18 201, in Roman numerals
19 "Don't worry!": 2 wds.
21 Large amount
22 It: It.
23 In concealment
25 Relating to old Norse poetry
27 Comic book heroine, ___ Queen of the Jungle
29 Raised platform
32 ___ Arann (Irish carrier)
33 Forage crop of the pea family
35 ___ Tuesday (Mardi Gras)
36 Golf course score
37 Delight
38 Get up
40 Often-missed humor
42 Sources
43 Joint on the foot
44 Otherwise: 2 wds.
45 Former Algerian rulers

Down

1 Wide-mouthed wine bottle
2 Gets used to
3 Aggressive promotion of one's views, etc.: hyph.
4 One past due
5 Salivary gland near the ear
6 Colorado native
7 Trick played on someone: 2 wds.
8 Summertime cooler, for short: 2 wds.
9 Providing relief
11 Org.
17 "Quelle surprise!": hyph.
20 Gardener's tool
24 "Baby ___ Bad Bad Thing" (Chris Isaak song): 2 wds.
26 Metrical foot in poetry
27 Hunting expedition
28 Learn about: 2 wds.
30 Phrase spoken with hindsight: 2 wds.
31 Yield: 2 wds.
34 Cerveza ___ (cold beer)
39 Pou ___, standing place
41 Boxing match div.

34

Across

1 Amount of hair gel
4 Alley animal
7 "___ Gang"
8 Egg cells
9 Dowel
12 Front-door sort
14 ___-Tzu (Chinese philosopher)
15 Haunted house sounds
16 Beauty queen's crown
18 Floating refuges
19 Limit intake
20 Didn't get used
21 First day of the month in Ancient Rome
24 Unfortunate
26 Chilled dessert
28 Cleopatra biter
31 Dwarf buffalo
32 Bit
33 180-degree reversal: hyph.
35 Bashes
36 Section, as of a race
37 Monkshood or wolfsbane
39 Blonde shade
40 Gold digger's prop
41 Buff
42 Cataract site
43 Fed. property overseer

Down

1 Beliefs
2 ___ borealis (northern lights)
3 Make a sudden advance
4 Camp beds
5 Monopoly property, often: abbr.
6 Bakery product
9 Easy, unobstructed progress: 2 wds.
10 Kind of seal
11 Fall guys
13 Lt.'s inferior, in the Navy
17 March 15, for example
21 Calculating person, for short
22 "Arabian Nights" name
23 Affranchise
25 At a distance
26 Comic Poundstone
27 Puts up, as 10 cents
29 Position
30 Bygone money
32 "Gee whiz!"
34 Back of the neck
35 Departed
38 Islet

35

Across

1 Black bird
4 Shag rug made in Sweden
7 Clandestine
10 Mythical being, half man and half horse
12 Lao-tzu's "way"
13 Young offenders' institution of old
15 Overdo a scene
16 Confidence game
17 Bottomless pits
19 Comic's Muse
22 Occurs, poetically
24 Cyst
25 "Walk ___ Line"
27 Instinctive
28 Former GM make, shortly
30 Mean and cranky
32 Capital of the island of Hokkaido
34 1000 dirhams in Libya
35 Like some colonies
39 Hard to control
41 Scrape by (with "out")
42 Major news media
43 Frank McCourt memoir
44 Tolkien beast
45 Collector's goal

Down

1 Farm division
2 Indian tree
3 It's gathered by scouts
4 Baked dish
5 "Dee-lish!"
6 Keffiyeh wearers
7 Earliest known period of human culture: 2 wds.
8 Plant of the buttercup family
9 It comes easily to hand: hyph.
11 Full amount
14 Pshaw
18 Country bumpkin
19 Double standard?
20 Capital of Finland
21 Moderately slow musical movements
23 Dump
26 Unpredictable
29 Go a few rounds
31 Cactus related to the prickly pear
33 Place to see some Goya paintings
34 Health regimen
36 Nile bird
37 Nautical direction
38 Cozy retreat
40 Cadillac or Porsche

36

Across

1 "Married at First Sight" network: 3 wds.
6 "He's ___ duck!": 2 wds.
11 Rest period
12 Esther ___, Florida Evans on "Maude"
13 Inflammation suffered by athletes: 2 wds.
15 "___ first you don't succeed…": 2 wds.
16 Cartoon bird
17 "The Woman ___" (Gene Wilder film): 2 wds.
19 Major record label, once
22 S.A. country
25 Certain wind
28 1972 treaty subj.
29 Insect with hard wing cases
30 Antler point
32 They're history
35 Shrek, for one
39 1972 hit for Carly Simon: 3 wds.
41 Sea birds
42 "___ of Athens" (Shakespeare)
43 ___ of time
44 Sample, as of food

Down

1 Italian wine area
2 Hebrew letter
3 1980s German pop star
4 Tooth doctor
5 Prefix with log or leptic
6 "___ nearly there yet?": 2 wds.
7 Meted (out)
8 North Sea feeder
9 Buckets: 2 wds.
10 Covered in morning moisture, as a meadow
14 Worker with responsibility but little authority, slangily: 2 wds.
18 Mathematician's ordinal
19 Fit ___ fiddle: 2 wds.
20 Steal
21 Ending for titan or thor
22 Letters in telecom
23 Fam. member
24 Test for a college sr.
26 Bard's nightfall
27 Spanish classical guitarist Andrés
30 Cut back
31 Like Boston accents, as it were: hyph.
32 Agreements at sea
33 "A Doll's House" heroine
34 "Cats" director Trevor
36 Pinup's legs
37 Protest in the streets
38 Feminine ending
40 Baseball's Mel

37

Across

1 Rattles
5 Condo cousin
9 Sheltered, at sea
10 Animals
11 Bellyache
12 Sable kin
13 Disease caused by a lack of thiamine
15 Lobster and beluga products
16 Distinctive flair
20 Bunny cousins
21 Kind of palm
22 Eternity, seemingly
23 High school class, for short
25 Dracula, at times
26 CGS units of work
28 Baseball blunder
30 "Trick" joint
31 Bad friend, e.g.
32 They're added as a bonus: hyph.
36 Prestige
39 Act the agitator
40 Kingsley film
41 Mercury, for one
42 It holds the team together
43 "Check this out!"

Down

1 Door holder
2 Burn balm
3 Place in a different order
4 High-ranking
5 Dental decay
6 At lunch, maybe
7 "___ Tree Hill"
8 Greek deity, a cross between a man and a goat
10 ___ cry
12 French men
14 BBC nickname, with "the"
17 Difficult
18 Gelatin substitute
19 "___ a chance"
20 Game ender, at times
22 "A rat!"
24 About: 2 wds.
27 Couch
29 Cover over
33 Be busy
34 Pesky insects
35 Coin depository
36 Hardly outgoing
37 Chinese "way"
38 Biblical floater

38

Across

1 Spotted cavy
5 Real estate ad abbr.
9 Gets on in years
10 Water nymph
11 Research facil.
12 Confused situation
13 Authors and such
15 Scientologist founder Hubbard: 2 wds.
16 Colleges, to Aussies
20 Country, capital Paris
22 Oliver Twist's request
23 Actresses Tyler or Ullmann
24 Kit ___ (candy bar)
26 Boy child
27 ___ were: 2 wds.
29 Burt Reynolds film of 1968
31 It may have a big head
32 O.K. Corral lawman Wyatt
33 Hangs on the line: hyph.
37 Prearranged situations: hyph.
40 Prefix with dynamic
41 Tomato blight
42 Long-running police drama series
43 Jane Austen character
44 Ten: prefix

Down

1 Sandbox toy
2 Vedic god of fire
3 Such is life, in France: 3 wds.
4 Rearward
5 Element drunk before an X-ray
6 One day in Spain
7 Manipuri dance form
8 Rx prescribers
10 "She loves me ___"
12 Some tigers and sharks, e.g.: hyph.
14 Hard ___ Cafe
17 Central part of a pair of glasses
18 Clothes presser
19 Dispatch
20 Exercise target
21 Greet the day
25 Football quarterback Lewis
28 Major shock to the system
30 Gofer's task
34 Beer variety, initially
35 Guitarist Clapton
36 Sammy of baseball fame
37 Get a good look at
38 Teacher's deg.
39 Pro ___ (for now)

39

Across

1 Stand for
6 Arcturus, for example: 2 wds.
11 Arrested: 2 wds.
12 In ___ (not yet born)
13 Extra
14 Life of luxury and pleasure, la ___ vita
15 Trevino and Harper
16 Cheek
17 Some sneakers
19 La-la lead-in
22 First stage of an operation: 2 wds.
24 "___ in alpha": 2 wds.
25 Bolt down
26 Small amount
28 Guitar master Paul
29 Meyers of "Kate & Allie"
30 Most recent
32 "Dungeons & Dragons," e.g.
33 Low-lying wetland
34 Antioxidant-rich berry
36 Prefix with graph
39 Work hard
41 Thinking organ
42 Apportion
43 Before the due date
44 "It's ___ Hard Day's Night" (Beatles song): 2 wds.
45 Capable of: 2 wds.

Down

1 Shrinking Asian sea
2 Commanded
3 Persisting tirelessly
4 Printing character: ‡
5 Conclusion
6 Acclaim
7 Pack away
8 Short story by Poe, "The ___": hyph., 2 wds.
9 Curved bit
10 Fish eggs
16 Game like pelota: 2 wds.
18 Directed
20 Dawn Chong and Carruth
21 Helper: abbr.
22 Liqueur flavor
23 Stringed instrument
27 Place to get some drinks
31 Woman's shoe feature: hyph.
33 "The She-Hulk Diaries" author Acosta
35 Masked critter, briefly
37 Cheery song
38 Greek war goddess
39 DNA testing facility
40 Brewed drink
41 Actress Benaderet

40

Across

1. ___ four
6. Molding at the base of a column
11. Circumvent
12. Alpine crest
13. Authorized
14. Physics lab device, for short
15. Thin canvas rug
17. Burnett or Channing
18. Clever tactic
21. One dozen
25. Suffix with mountain or musket
26. "We ___ to please"
27. Reddish-brown color
31. Edible roots
32. W.W. I soldier
34. Place for extra passengers in a small car: 2 wds.
39. Big house
40. Central, open areas
41. Dispatch boat
42. Musical "repeat" sign
43. Big name in oil
44. Moves briskly

Down

1. Ill-gotten gains
2. Diabolical
3. Food in a shell
4. Foolishness
5. "Four" at the fore
6. Fat used for making soap
7. Baltimore bird
8. 1996 Tony-winning musical
9. 2002 Winter Olympics locale
10. Dry, as wine
16. Computer monitor, for short
18. Podded plant
19. Moldovan monetary unit
20. Ball
22. Anita Brookner's "Hotel du ___"
23. ___ Appia
24. Bad ___, German resort
28. Highest
29. Manhattan cocktail made with Scotch whisky: 2 wds.
30. It's really nothing
31. Dismissal, expulsion
33. Minimal
34. 1990s party
35. ___ cost
36. "Cogito, ___ sum"
37. Is not on the street?
38. Art colony of New Mexico
39. Glossy publication, for short

41

Across

1 Others, in Madrid
6 ___ example: 2 wds.
11 French W.W. I soldier
12 "Educating Rita" actor Michael
13 See-through
15 Partner of poivre
16 Sweltering
17 Loosen up hemp
18 Piece of body art, briefly
19 Ending for real or classical
20 Suffix with rep or rev
21 Platte River people
23 Bicycle seat
25 Elaborate solo in opera
27 Official documents
30 Celebrity
34 Enzyme ending
35 Bear, in Bolivia
37 Ceremonious verse
38 Geographical abbr.
39 Get spliced
40 Sounds of disbelief
41 Long and harsh questioning, to obtain information: 2 wds.
44 Overplay a role
45 Far from lenient
46 Put on, as cargo
47 Start of a comparison involving a beet: 2 wds.

Down

1 Makes a decision: 2 wds.
2 Attacked violently: 2 wds.
3 Old theater name
4 Former name of the cable network Versus, initially
5 Raw fish dish
6 "Louie the Garbage Man" actor Crothers
7 Head attachment
8 In layers
9 Temper, as metal
10 Irk
14 Had ownership
22 Atlanta to Miami dir.
24 Court figures, initially
26 Packed like sardines
27 Pale (of colour)
28 Breathing problem
29 Portion of time
31 Bygone auto
32 Cling (to)
33 Try again, as to deliver an e-mail
36 Black Sea port, new-style
42 A1A, I65, or 66, e.g.
43 Fast sports cars, for short

42

Across

1 In ___ (mad): 2 wds.
6 Fairy-bluebird genus
11 Piece goods, perhaps
12 Taboos: hyph.
13 Municipal pound employees: 2 wds.
15 Balancing pro letters
16 "___-te-Ching"
17 ___ Tin Tin
18 Capacity of many a flash drive, informally: 2 wds.
20 Brit. gasolene
23 Barely beats
26 "Please have ___": 2 wds.
27 Hitlerites
28 Mia of U.S. soccer
29 Secretary of Transportation under Bush
30 Classic theater name
32 Affirmative vote
34 An N.Y.C. subway
35 Be worthwhile
38 Travel very fast: 2 wds.
41 1985 movie starring Kate Nelligan
42 Jay Silverheels role
43 "No mas!" boxer
44 Respected one

Down

1 Aussie hard-rock band
2 Food for pigs
3 Robe for Caesar
4 "Yadda, yadda, yadda"
5 Nondescript article
6 In disguise: abbr.
7 "Ruh-___!" (Scooby-Doo phrase)
8 Stimulate
9 Seaweed, in sushi bars
10 NBA part
14 Former Chinese monetary unit
18 Humorous ending meaning "big amount of"
19 Absurd
20 "Fiddlesticks!"
21 That, in Spanish
22 Modifying agent
24 Center of a peach
25 F.I.C.A. funds it
27 Wink: var.
29 Clay-sand mixture
31 ___ wait: 2 wds.
32 Sacked out
33 Korea Bay feeder
35 Lake's little cousin
36 ___ meridiem
37 "Son of Frankenstein" shepherd
39 Biochemistry abbr.
40 "Hilarious," to texters

43

Across

1 Fable writer
6 Northern subarctic coniferous forest
11 Squalid residences
12 All, in stage directions
13 French royal name
14 Agreements between nations
15 Doing business
16 "I'll ___ for Christmas": 2 wds.
17 Early role-playing game co., initially
18 Blacken
19 "Life is Good" rapper
20 ___ Heaney, poet who penned "North"
22 Certain boxer shorts
23 "I haven't a clue": 2 wds.
25 Small flake of soot
27 Flavored sugar toppings
30 Summer shade
31 Luau serving
32 Summer Games gp.
33 Appends: 2 wds.
35 St. Petersburg's river
36 Grain husks
37 Stupid mistake
38 Strips of track for swimmers
39 Start of a French oath
40 Lauder of perfume
41 Edit

Down

1 Broad silk neckties
2 Pass, as time
3 More than sufficient
4 Augur's concern
5 San Diego setting: abbr.
6 Sot
7 Indian nursemaid
8 Difficulty that causes anxiety
9 Lose your temper: 2 wds.
10 Rate
16 Group that defends a principle
18 Douro river tributary
21 Came across
22 Weight to height ratio, initially
24 ___-fi
25 Home to a horse
26 Former name for Chennai, India
28 Regulate
29 Fearful
31 Search party
34 Old knife
35 "Occupy" author Chomsky
37 Jamboree grp.

44

Across

1 Dog
6 "___ for the way you look at me" (line from a song): 2 wds.
9 End of some plays
11 "First of all…"
12 Greek
14 Fight club, initially
15 Tooth-doctors' org.
16 Financial regulators, initially
17 "All the King's Men" star Joanne
18 Bend in ship's timber
19 Bubbler
21 "Lost" setting: abbr.
22 ___ function
23 Very expensive, slangily: hyph.
26 Church, poetically
27 #s
28 Diva's problem
30 P.I., e.g.
33 ___ Nabisco (former corporation name)
34 Griffin Dunne comedy, "___ Service"
35 "___ Adore" (1997 Smashing Pumpkins single)
36 16 1/2 feet
37 5th-century Germanic leader
39 "Can ___ dreaming?": 2 wds.
40 Accompany
41 Kazakhstan letters, once
42 Café cup

Down

1 Laughter sounds
2 Indian, for one
3 Chase of the Phillies
4 Zero, in soccer scores
5 Molded, as metal
6 It may clash with the rest of the suit: 2 wds.
7 Ahead: 2 wds.
8 Safe
10 Computer chip slogan: 2 wds.
13 Ring bearer, maybe
20 Responds correctly on "Jeopardy!"
21 "___ Around" (Beach Boys' song): 2 wds.
23 Spy's break-ins, in slang: 2 wds.
24 Called for: 2 wds.
25 Gardener's supply
26 Kind of wheel
29 Labor group initials
30 Mexican food, sometimes
31 "Tinker to ___ to Chance" (Franklin Pierce Adams poem)
32 Bill of fare
38 Here, in Mexico

45

Across

1 Breaks for most of the players
6 Indigo-yielding shrubs
11 Oil can, maybe
12 Of certain ecological areas
13 "That's ___ nonsense!"
14 Dirt
15 "Aladdin" prince
16 Diamonds, to hoods
18 Old Tokyo
19 "Argo" director Affleck
20 Loire valley product
21 Beret or beanie
22 Crosspieces between the legs of a chair
24 Additionally
25 Chess pieces
26 "The Princess and the ___"
27 Alpine animal
29 Corps member
32 Hide-hair link
33 More, in Madrid
34 Sun follower?
35 ___ generis (unique)
36 Decide to leave, with "out"
37 Build (on)
38 Bring upon oneself
40 Permeate
42 Cornrow's place
43 Islamic teacher: var.
44 Like John Tyler, among presidents
45 Arab leader: var.

Down

1 Young pigeons
2 Bargain hunter's heaven
3 Mexican, e.g.: hyph.
4 State that "Portlandia" is filmed in: abbr.
5 Tried hard
6 Colorado ski resort, or a tree you might find there
7 Keanu Reeves's character in "The Matrix"
8 Insusceptible of reform
9 Martin of "Ed Wood"
10 Boats with one mast
17 Alliance that includes Russia, Tajikistan, Moldova, etc.
23 Annoy
24 The "p" in r.p.m.
26 Hobby
27 Put one's foot down
28 ___ back (recover)
29 AAA offering
30 Tubercle
31 Make liked
33 Shift shape
39 Last, for short
41 Ornamental flower, for short

46

Across

1 Humorist
4 Bag
7 ___ Darya (Asian river)
10 Soccer's Freddy or Fro
11 Earthshaking?
13 Act like a sauna operator?: 3 wds.
15 French wolf
16 Black gunk
17 Male cat
20 Relatives
23 One of the Ramones: 2 wds.
26 Middle grade
27 Bridal ring: 2 wds.
29 Year in Edward the Elder's reign
30 "Seinfeld" lady
31 Chesterfield, e.g.
33 "___ Black Magic"
34 Cyclones' sch.
36 ___ dawn: 2 wds.
40 Elated
44 Mrs. Franklin Roosevelt
45 Chinese ideal
46 More, in Managua
47 Sun Devils' sch.
48 Down units: abbr.

Down

1 Barrier
2 Prefix with gram
3 Ballet skirt
4 Bouncing letters
5 W.W. I army, initially
6 "Bei Mir ___ Du Schön"
7 Like apple pie
8 Lamb's cry
9 City on the Danube
12 Train stops: abbr.
14 ___ out (declined)
18 "Garfield" dog
19 ___ Park, N.J.
21 The "B" of N.B.
22 But, to a Roman
23 Kind of tape
24 Buildings
25 Alike, in Paris
27 Johns in Britain: abbr.
28 Cause to get higher, as a price at auction: 2 wds.
32 "___ silly question…": 2 wds.
35 Arm part
37 Feel sorry for
38 Run ___ in the paper: 2 wds.
39 Bout enders, for short
40 President pro ___
41 Dockworker's org.
42 Dawn deity
43 R&B band ___ Hill

47

Across

1 Part of a TV
4 Compete in the Winter Olympics, maybe
7 Monte Viso, e.g.
10 "___ Miss Brooks"
11 "___ folly to be wise"
12 ___-Impressionism (art movement)
13 Floral necklace
14 ___ gland (epinephrine secreter)
16 Get better, often
18 "Home ___" (1990 movie)
19 Moldovan monetary unit
20 Australian bird
21 Fellas
23 "Twin Peaks" co-creator David
26 Charge carrier
27 Dove's sound
28 Befuddle
31 Encircle as a military tactic
33 Precambrian, for instance
34 "We ___ to please"
35 Make a rhythmic sound
37 Amphitheater levels
40 When the show must go on
42 Rob Roy's refusal
43 Con balancer
44 Foot "finger"
45 Demolition stuff, shortly
46 Always, to a poet
47 Pointer's direction

Down

1 Pepsi, for one
2 Bemoaned
3 Experimentation: 3 wds.
4 Condition
5 Joke around
6 David, "the sweet psalmist of ___"
7 Formal public statement
8 Low-fat
9 Fishing need
15 Abounding in shade trees
17 ___ rally (high school event)
21 Bush Sr. once headed it
22 Mason's burden
24 Gear tooth
25 Unharden the garden, in a way
29 Churlish sort
30 Ill will
31 Cotton fabric with a shiny finish
32 "Rocky ___"
35 Cash register part
36 Add to the staff
38 Competed
39 Three of a kind, in poker
41 Calf's laugh

48

Across

1 G.P. grp.
4 Stock letters
7 ___ Simbel, Egypt
10 Go-___ (1980s band)
11 Style of enunciation in speaking
13 Hollow wooden statue of Greek myth: 2 wds.
15 Living room piece
16 Facing: abbr.
17 Genetic stuff, for short
20 Flat piece
23 Whizzes
26 Cable inits.
27 Stupid in an annoying way: hyph.
29 Here, in France
30 Campanologist
31 Celtic god of the boar
33 Rep. or Dem., e.g.
34 Heartbeat record, for short
36 Notice of departure
40 Nursery rhyme bird: 2 wds.
44 "The Mary Tyler Moore Show" costar: 2 wds.
45 Spelling competition
46 B.S., e.g.
47 Dental org.
48 Wine: prefix

Down

1 PR people: abbr.
2 Aldo ___, former Italian P.M.
3 From that time: 2 wds.
4 "Sweet as apple cider" girl
5 Bowling target
6 Eight, in Havana
7 Powered flying vehicle
8 Diddley and Derek
9 French article
12 Spinning toys
14 Worn out
18 Wyo. neighbor
19 Leaking
21 Continental abbr.
22 Alphabet trio
23 Film director Vittorio De ___
24 Sticker on goods for sale: 2 wds.
25 Not loco
27 Baby's protector
28 Arctic abode
32 Newspaper publisher Adolph
35 Rowlands of "The Notebook"
37 "The ___" (Peter Sellers movie of 1967)
38 Psychiatrist's reply: 2 wds.
39 Adolescent
40 It's not quite lge.
41 Poetic form
42 New Deal inits.
43 Educ. test

49

Across

1 Sleeve ends
6 #1 spot
10 Green
12 Big loser's nickname?
13 Blue pencil wielder
14 Angel's headwear
15 Landscaper's need
16 Outer space sphere, like the sun or moon
18 Be in session
19 Unshorn sheep
20 Brief peek, slangily: hyph.
22 A, in geometry
24 Medical research monkey
25 Media watchdog agcy.
27 Abbr. after some generals' names
28 Sleeping car features
31 Prefix with fall
34 Reflexive pronoun
36 Revulsion remark
37 Took the cake, say
38 Highlands negative
39 "Oh, wow!"
40 King or queen, e.g.
42 Fly larva
44 Difficult journey
45 ___ Artois (beer brand)
46 Arid
47 Mushers' vehicles

Down

1 Spanish hill
2 Cause for a downfall
3 Kitchen appliance: hyph.
4 Appropriate
5 Yo-yo, essentially
6 ___ blond
7 Civil strife: 2 wds.
8 Setting
9 Chews the scenery
11 "I don't understand," to computers
17 Atomic physicist Niels ___
21 Castle part
23 Book before Romans
26 Julie, "Big Brother" host
28 Crows
29 Aggregate
30 Scathing insults
32 Ancient: hyph.
33 Some sorority women
35 Accomplishments
41 Barely make, with "out"
43 Salon stuff

50

Across

1 Bitter feeling
4 Be mistaken
7 Driver's license datum
8 Anonymous John or Jane
9 Center of a ball?
12 Baseball great Mel
13 Non-Jew
15 Revel
17 Or, musically
18 "Fine with me"
19 Mine shafts
20 Sack
24 After expenses
25 Keep going
27 Black and tan beverage
29 Symbolic devices
32 "Goldberg Variations" composer
34 Curved molding
35 Pipe material
37 Not domesticated
38 Slippery
40 ___ right
41 Jack's "On the Road" alter ego
42 Flipper
43 50–50, e.g.
44 Little 'un
45 Ballad ending

Down

1 Kind of crustacean
2 Second shot
3 Exceptionally good: hyph.
4 Hardly cool
5 Caviar
6 Betting setting
9 Fall to pieces
10 Beautiful people
11 Savage
14 Dosage amt.
16 Pound a keyboard
21 Taconite, e.g.
22 Belief system
23 Freedom, briefly
26 ___-eyed
27 French clerics
28 Cocoon contents
30 South African maize plant
31 Vendor
33 Controls
36 Break in friendly relations
37 Provide (for oneself)
39 ___ Appia

51

Across

1 Banned chemical compound
4 Medical amts.
7 "I get it!"
8 Ostracized person
13 "Regnava ___ silenzio" (aria from "Lucia di Lammermoor")
14 Full to satisfaction
15 "The Sound of Music" family name
17 Hutchinson and Candler
18 One, in Vienna
19 Expel from a country
21 Sound intensity unit
23 Latin foot
24 Place to catch game highlights: 2 wds.
26 "For ___ a jolly good fellow..."
28 Accepted member of our group: 3 wds.
31 Actress Judd
33 Cooper's "High Noon" role
34 Lawsuit beneficiary
35 Composer of "Euryanthe"
36 ___ Mutant Ninja Turtles
39 Delay
40 Authorize
41 Ending for Vietnam or Siam
42 Police officer
43 Due + due + due

Down

1 Gasped for breath
2 Stevie Wonder hit, "My ___ Amour"
3 Financial statement of a company: 2 wds.
4 Large grp. of businesses
5 It gets chalked between shots
6 Indy sponsor, initially
9 Applaud
10 "The Hare and the Tortoise," "The Monkey as King," "The Fox and the Crow," etc.: 2 wds.
11 Gawk (at)
12 Exams
16 Trident-shaped letters
19 1963 Jr. Middleweight Champion of the World, ___ Moyer
20 Part of a C.S.A. signature: 2 wds.
22 Fraternal gp.
25 Aroused
26 Like some cuisine
27 City near Düsseldorf
29 Feeling of discomfort
30 Composer Rachmaninov
32 Filmmaker Riefenstahl
35 Cry
37 Airport service letters
38 ___ Worm (old Playskool toy)

52

Across

1 Swamp
5 Ran off to get married
11 Flat: hyph.
12 "___ Butterfly" (Puccini opera)
13 Singer, dancer, comedian, e.g.
15 Serta competitor
16 Johnnycake basis
17 Part of H.R.H.
18 ___ de toilette
21 Home of the Bulldogs, initially
22 Extra: abbr.
24 Of a grayish color
26 Spreadsheet cell contents
28 1966 U.S. Open champion Fred
31 "___ and away!": 2 wds.
35 Pitcher's pride
36 Set of functions in computing, initially
38 John Lennon's love
39 Kin of hic or hoc
41 Loses color
43 Magician
46 Actors Bucklind and Noah
47 Fungal spore sacs
48 Take up residence
49 Discharged a firearm

Down

1 Former UPN sitcom series
2 Poverty stricken: 2 wds.
3 Hold back
4 Henry James biographer Leon
5 Hosp. employee
6 When doubled, a Teletubby
7 Lyrical
8 Prove successful: 2 wds.
9 Come to light
10 Charles ___, "A Tale of Two Cities" character
14 Bread often used in delis
19 "___ From Heaven" (first novel by An Na)
20 "The Deep End of the Ocean" director Grosbard
23 "Bad" cholesterol carrier
25 ___ Darya (Asian river)
27 Menu phrase: 2 wds.
28 Indian gentlemen
29 County Kerry capital of song
30 Frittata
32 Make smooth and shiny
33 Maintainer of the World Heritage List
34 Sticky note brand: hyph.
37 Wall Street operation, for short
40 Abrupt
42 Collections of anecdotes
44 Blues and soul singer Johnson
45 British verb suffix

53

Across

1 Foreign Legion hat
5 Crops up
11 "___ (For You Baby)" (Ritchie family song): 4 wds.
13 Classic breakfast: 2 wds.
14 One laying down sticky stuff
15 Boundary: comb. form
16 ___-dink
20 Grammy category: abbr., 3 wds.
21 Chalon-sur-___, city SSW of Dijon
22 High-on-the-highway letters
23 Bleed
24 Indian state
27 Brad and William, e.g.
29 ___ music (compose a score for): 2 wds.
30 Tennis champ Arthur
31 Large soft hat of old
33 They're made on January 1st
38 Dish with lettuce, cheese and croutons: 2 wds.
39 Indifference
40 Half in front?

Down

1 Laotian money
2 "Hold on Tight" band, initially
3 Aristotle, for one
4 Bouncer's check: 2 wds.
5 Certain league: abbr.
6 Actress Winona and others
7 1968 James Michener novel
8 Circle pt.
9 Monogram of Mason mysteries' author
10 MA and PA
12 Laura Petrie's anguished cry: 2 wds.
15 Hole that an anchor rope passes through
17 End of the world?: 2 wds.
18 "All American" name
19 Aches (for)
20 Vitamin amts.
25 Not more than: 2 wds.
26 Simoleons
27 Agreements
28 Jeremiah preceder
32 Cover completely
33 "His Master's Voice" initials
34 Literary monogram
35 Bering, for one
36 "China Beach" setting, in short
37 "Star Wars" project of the 1980s

54

Across

1 Silk-producing region of India
6 Autumn toiler
11 Arch or mony lead-in
12 To love, Italian style
13 City in northern Portugal
14 Fork projections
15 Jared of "Panic Room"
16 Big name in small planes
17 Loafer designation
18 Place for a drink
19 Big screen letters
20 Couch potatoes' perches
22 Life ___ know it: 2 wds.
23 Tracy Chapman hit of 1988: 2 wds.
25 "___ girl!"
27 Turkish money
29 "Well, ___-di-dah!"
30 Crime-busters' grp.
31 Cyclades island
33 Circus sites
35 1998 Sarah McLachlan ballad
36 Actor Keach
37 Yanks and Sox, briefly
38 Fashion designer Donna
39 Daughter of Saturn
40 Cavern, in poetry
41 Actor Affleck

Down

1 Walk casually
2 Hindu dresses
3 Highest level of development: 4 wds.
4 Jason's ship, in myth
5 Actress Farrow
6 Appraiser
7 "The Old Devils" author
8 1950 movie with Tony Curtis and Audie Murphy: 2 wds.
9 Before the present: 2 wds.
10 Flea market deal
16 Beach houses?
18 ___-relief
21 Airline overseer, initially
22 Rhine feeder
24 Subject of Tom Clancy's "The Good Shepherd"
25 49th state
26 Kilt pattern
28 Evening engagement
30 Pop singer Taylor
32 Fresh-mouthed
34 Neighbor of Tenn.: 2 wds.
35 Greek goddess Athena ___
37 Banking abbr.

55

Across

1 Musical symbol: 2 wds.
6 Tool for bending metal
11 Laborare est ___ (Masonic motto)
12 Dragged, historically
13 Tiny time period
15 That, in Oaxaca
16 Break
17 1,002, in old Rome
18 It borders Fla.
19 Flat-screens, e.g.
20 Tooth-doctors' org.
21 Just so: 3 wds.
23 WWW addresses
24 Ford flop
26 P.I.s
29 Letter-shaped band on a shoe: hyph.
33 All-purpose truck, for short
34 Alliance that includes Russia, Tajikistan, Moldova, etc.
35 Mo. in which the Civil War began
36 "Monster" rock group
37 Gallic soul
38 Extinct bird
39 Sustainable source of power: 2 wds.
42 Inspector Appleby's creator Michael
43 Aussie shout
44 "Star Wars" droid Artoo-___
45 ___ Wiggin (protagonist of Orson Scott Card novels)

Down

1 Approach: 2 wds.
2 The Count of Monte ___
3 Random chorus syllables: 3 wds.
4 Schubert's "The ___-King"
5 Faked, as in boxing
6 Some guard dogs, for short
7 SPAR's counterpart
8 Baseball family name
9 Agreeable
10 Whirlpools
14 Uses a shortcut: 2 wds.
22 French possessive
23 Final: abbr.
25 Gist
26 Bombastic
27 Everlasting, to the bard
28 Building material
30 Musket accessory
31 High point
32 Message communicated to God
34 Playground retort: 2 wds.
40 Classified ad letters
41 Long period of time

56

Across

1 TV teaser: abbr.
6 Lab chemical dropper
11 Poker champ Stu
12 Arab leader: var.
13 Singer who played Hattie Pearl in "The Butler": 2 wds.
15 Widow in "Peer Gynt"
16 Riga denizen
17 One of the Spice Girls
18 Bill amt.
21 Extremely inflexible: hyph.
23 Asia's Trans ___ mountains
25 Dudley Do-Right's gp.
26 Mexican border language
30 Opposite of a ques.
31 "Give ___ further thought!": 2 wds.
32 "Tomb raider" Croft
33 Sleep attire, briefly
36 Having no awareness
40 Absorbed the cost of a contract, slangily: 2 wds.
41 Firth of Clyde island
42 Partner of wheres and whys
43 Church engagement announcement

Down

1 Mountain lion
2 Genetic strands, initially
3 Fairy-tale character
4 ___ tai (rum cocktail)
5 Word-of-mouth bettor
6 Jelly ingredient
7 "Where ___" (Eminem song): 2 wds.
8 ___ annum
9 Ample shoe width
10 "Don't give up!"
14 Bunch of bulls
17 Acquire
18 Function used in arrays
19 ___ and haw
20 Measure of an economy, initially
21 Lukas of "Rambling Rose"
22 About: 2 wds.
23 ___ rule: 2 wds.
24 Home care provider, initially
27 New York footballers
28 Posts: abbr.
29 Occupying a taxi: 3 wds.
32 Cut of meat
33 V-chips block it
34 Evita's hubby
35 Form 1040 IDs
36 Bob King's org.
37 ___ power
38 Bee follower
39 401(k) alternative

57

Across

1 Large motor vehicles
6 Indo-European
11 Allocute
12 "Northern Exposure" creature
13 Boxing category
15 Juice berry
16 Some woodwork designs
17 Small room on a boat
19 On fire
22 "7 Faces of Dr. ___"
25 Instrument played by the wind: 2 wds.
28 Cut, as a tree
29 Clan members
30 Ism
32 Owner's guidebook
35 Barber's job
39 Involving deduction of theories from facts: 2 wds.
41 Extra inning
42 Take off a diaper, e.g.
43 Hair piece
44 Externalize, in a way

Down

1 Gaucho's weapon
2 Acid related to gout
3 Epic
4 Aboveboard
5 Arrange
6 Change, as the Constitution
7 Muddy, turbulent
8 Practice with a "lotus position"
9 Begrimed with soot
10 Brings home
14 Lens for a panoramic shot
18 Arm of Israel?
19 "Ooh! ___!"
20 Contest involving letters
21 Coolest temperature of the day
22 Anita Brookner's "Hotel du ___"
23 "How ___ things today?"
24 Photo-___ (politician's events): abbr.
26 Matchsticks game
27 Bringing to a high temperature
30 Covers with a powdered substance
31 Presidential affirmations
32 Actor Damon of "Rounders" and "The Bourne Ultimatum"
33 Little, e.g.
34 "With malice toward ___ ..." (Lincoln)
36 Catch, in a way
37 Camera part
38 Coin factory
40 Street, on some New Orleans signs

58

Across

1 Habituate: var.
6 Following
11 City in Kentucky
12 Dry Italian white wine
13 Goes off, as a timer
14 Seoul's home
15 Stings a little bit
17 Hall near the quad
18 Bar, legally
20 Big do
23 Medicinal plant
27 Architectural projection
29 Patterned fabric
30 Sawbuck
32 Secret language
33 Taste, touch or sight
35 LP player: hyph.
38 Reply
42 Building block
44 City on Honshu
45 Chap
46 Thesaurus compiler
47 Selfish person
48 Head lock

Down

1 Goes back, like the tide
2 Margosa tree
3 Common fertilizer ingredient
4 Deserving severe rebuke or censure
5 Bridge positions
6 Establish, as a price
7 Kitchen appliance: 2 wds.
8 Poi source
9 Anytime
10 500 sheets
16 Farm pen
19 Cracklin' ___ Bran
20 Computerized task performer
21 "Butterflies ___ Free"
22 Transgression
24 Brazil resort, familiarly
25 As ___ as the hills
26 Diminutive
28 Linda ___, Supergirl's alias
31 Genetic messenger material, briefly
34 Haughty response
35 Dagger grip
36 Cogitation creation
37 People
39 Hourly pay
40 Just makes, with "out"
41 "Gosh darn it!"
43 Attention, metaphorically

59

Across

1 Printers' widths
4 Music from Jamaica
7 Engage in espionage
10 Palindromic woman's name
11 World ___ II
12 Paris' ___ de la Cité
13 Customary
16 Go out
17 I.R.A. part: abbr.
18 Movie parts
19 Lets go
20 Nutmeg-based spice
22 Diamond stat.
23 Twin killings, in baseball, initially
26 Confederate general
27 Almost forever
28 Fury
29 Ill-gotten gains
31 George Eliot miser Marner
33 Become established: 2 wds.
37 "Holy ___, that's a surprise!"
38 Spanish dance in triple time
39 National barrier between the Soviet bloc and the West: 2 wds.
41 Actor Gilliam
42 Bull's-eye: abbr.
43 ___-Cat (winter vehicle)
44 Drunkard
45 Produce eggs
46 Federal warning system, initially

Down

1 Keyboard key
2 Bette Davis's role in "All About Eve"
3 Tangle
4 Mountainous region of Europe: 2 wds.
5 Kit ___ (candy bars)
6 Mr. Onassis
7 Heartfelt
8 Innocuous or inert medication
9 Former president of the Russian Federation
14 Make a judgment
15 Paddle's cousin
19 Suffer remorse: 2 wds.
21 Copyright letter
23 Reject
24 Before: 2 wds.
25 Betrayal for reasons of expedience: 2 wds.
30 Sensed
32 Rand who wrote "The Fountainhead"
34 Flirt with
35 Russian woman's name
36 Things not to do: hyph.
38 "You Ain't Nothing ___ Hound Dog" (Presley song): 2 wds.
40 Half of D, to a Roman

60

Across

1 Tag ___ with
6 Certain fraction
11 Go through
12 Atlanta research university
13 Allude
14 Consume: 2 wds.
15 "___ luck?"
16 Common connector
18 QVC rival
19 G.I. entertainers
20 Light units: abbr.
21 Honshu city
22 DOT, alternatively
24 "The ___ Love": 2 wds.
25 Antique shop item
27 Looked for over the intercom
28 About, on a memo: 2 wds.
29 Embarrassing info, to the tabloids
30 General on a Chinese menu
31 Brief time, briefly
32 "___ Buttermilk Sky" (Hoagy Carmichael song)
35 Takeoff and landing overseers, initially
36 Common deciduous tree
37 Chat room initials
38 Senegal's capital
40 Smelly smoke
42 Cast out
43 Saharan sanctuary
44 Ancient Greeks' harps
45 Bridget Fonda, to Jane

Down

1 Pianist Claudio
2 Encumbrances
3 Nuts: 3 wds.
4 Nationals grp.
5 Talk show host Rivera
6 Demands
7 "___ little teapot…": 2 wds.
8 What a desperate person has: 3 wds.
9 Part of a board
10 Trance-like "state"
17 Macadamia or cashew
23 "Sprechen ___ deutsch?"
24 Dinghy propeller
25 Stronghold
26 Natural
27 Harasses: 2 wds.
29 Crime-busters' grp.
31 Puts into piles
33 Reasoned judgement
34 "Family Ties" mom
39 Enzyme ending
41 ___ chi (Chinese exercise)

61

Across

1 Beak
5 Ares, for one: 2 wds.
11 Hard on the eye
12 Any Smith grad.
13 "___ Grit" (1969 John Wayne film)
14 Austere
15 Lowly laborer
16 Barbie's guy
17 Geller feller
19 Thanksgiving dish
23 Implemented
27 Monetary unit of Romania
28 Ballpark figure, colloquially
30 Baseball number
31 Minnelli musical
32 Narcissist's love
34 Hallucinogen's initials
35 100 qintars
37 1996 also-ran
41 Game expedition
44 Bright thought
45 Surfing, perhaps
46 December drinks
47 Does salon work
48 Cave, to a poet

Down

1 Hard fruits
2 Beast
3 Bit of slander
4 Good looks
5 Precursors of cell phones: hyph.
6 Away from the wind
7 Semi-liquid
8 Clock std.
9 ___ in a million
10 Brown or Marino
18 Computer architecture, initially
20 Banned apple reddener
21 Deal (out)
22 Beef fat used in cooking
23 Countless years
24 Contaminant-free
25 Resound
26 "I call it!"
29 "Far From the ___ Crowd" (Hardy novel)
33 Swing wildly
36 Coastal flyer
38 Distinct smell
39 ___-mutton: hyph.
40 90 degrees
41 "Help!" letters
42 Tiny crawler
43 Birds do it

62

Across

1 Cause of septicemia: abbr.
6 ___ and blood (kin)
11 Life of ___
12 Really slow, on sheet music
13 A spoken curse
15 Bow
16 S. ___ (st. whose capital is Pierre)
17 Appear
20 Dance, music, etc.
22 Bearded bloomer
24 Language of southeastern India
28 Lower number in a vulgar fraction
30 Takes an oath
31 Farm building
32 "Aye" voters
34 "___ a Liar" (song by the Bee Gees)
35 Gangster's gun, for short
38 Creep
40 Overstated
45 Change, sci-fi style
46 Palatal pendant
47 Condescending one
48 Flexible

Down

1 ___ Lanka (country near India)
2 "Ed Wood" director Burton
3 Mont Blanc, e.g.
4 Exec's benefit
5 Animal known for its laugh
6 Make level
7 Release, with "out"
8 "Idylls of the King" lady
9 Ancient gathering place
10 Toot the horn
14 Steroid hormone
17 Assists
18 All hands on deck
19 Food sticker
21 Chunk or hunk
23 "General Hospital," e.g.
25 Its motto is "Industry"
26 Blood's partner
27 Caterer's collection
29 Perfect future husband: 2 wds.
33 Cancel
35 Beauties
36 Impulse transmitter
37 Member of the arum family
39 "___ a good one"
41 Agency providing printing for Congress, initially
42 252 wine gallons
43 Antiquity, once
44 86,400 seconds

63

Across

1 Cereal staple
5 Prevented from speaking out
11 Dab with absorbent paper
12 Burrowing rodent
13 "Field of Dreams" setting
14 Shade
15 Guard
17 "Absolutely!"
18 Deity with cow's horns
22 Compensate for
24 Classic color for stationery
25 Frog-dissecting class, for short
26 Pistol, slangily
27 Angled annexes
29 Church plates
32 Bind
33 From the beginning
34 Causing desire
38 Anatomical cavities
41 Canaanite deity
42 Domestic: 2 wds.
43 "___ for the poor"
44 Fishes with a dragnet
45 Delight

Down

1 Eastern ties
2 ___ vera (lotion ingredient)
3 Municipality dwellers
4 Condition
5 Large seabird
6 Bad fit?
7 Hands-on soccer player
8 Colt, e.g.
9 Abbr. after a comma
10 Backgammon cube
16 Anger
19 Wiggy
20 "Pumping ___"
21 Beer, casually
22 "Do as I say"
23 Flaky pastry
28 "Two for the ___," Gibson play
29 Flat stones
30 "Wheel of Fortune" buy: 2 wds.
31 It steeps in hot water: 2 wds.
35 Catch
36 "You can do better than that"
37 "... or ___!"
38 ___ Tuesday (Mardi Gras)
39 "___ Father"
40 "Fat" farm

64

Across

1 They could be in your favor
5 Door fixture
9 King in the "Iliad"
10 Culture mediums
12 Bridal path?
13 Trio, tripled
14 Bluecoat
15 Powerful hallucinogen, initially
17 Bug
18 Rubber band
20 Cheat, slangily
21 Take five, say
22 Proper address for a lady, in France
24 Pants presser of yore
26 Corkscrew
28 Alternative to nude
31 "The ___ of Pooh"
32 Muscular tremors
34 "A League of Their ___"
35 Voting "yes"
36 "___ Loves You"
37 Cry like a cat: var.
39 Arise
41 Cave
42 Zen riddles with no solution
43 Military leaders: abbr.
44 ___ of Solomon

Down

1 Baltimore ballplayer
2 Unaffected by strong emotion
3 Tex. city
4 Refine, as metal
5 Light railway vehicle
6 Back when
7 Certain Californian native: 2 wds.
8 Early round, for short
9 Indiana ballplayer
11 Bonehead
16 Nearly alike
19 Antares, for one
23 Impersonates
25 Marks with spots of shade
26 Leaf opening
27 Scraping the ground, as with a hoof
29 Moved the picture to a different room, e.g.
30 Computer operators
33 Sees
38 Ashes holder
40 Murmur

65

Across

1 ABC rival
4 Round, green vegetable
7 In what way?
8 Account
9 "Understand?"
12 Showy flower
14 Father, to Huck Finn
15 Like helium
16 Close call
18 Things to pick
19 Face cream target
20 All prepared
21 Angelina Jolie, for example
24 Catered gatherings
26 Colors for an artist
28 Check
31 Go for
32 Serpent deity group, in Hinduism
33 Cockeyed
35 "Psycho" setting
36 Perfect score, sometimes
37 Form a mental image
39 Physics class unit
40 Magnum, for one, slangily
41 "___ to Liberty" by Shelley
42 Bleating belle
43 A Bobbsey twin

Down

1 Metal shackles
2 Gangsters ___ and Clyde
3 Flattering persuasively: hyph.
4 Connive
5 Many, many moons
6 "It's been ___!"
9 Salut 1 was the first of its kind: 2 wds.
10 Brings home
11 Fencing swords
13 "The Ghost and ___ Muir"
17 "The Alienist" author Caleb
21 Back at sea?
22 Animal that meows
23 Make equal, as the score
25 Club dues
26 Dish
27 Pointer
29 Something hidden, perhaps
30 Whalebone
32 Egg ___ (Christmas concoction)
34 Construction location
35 Defensive spray
38 Kitten's cry

66

Across

1 Type measurements
6 Flippant
10 Mix socially
12 Bill of fare
13 Suggesting indirectly or obliquely
15 "Newsweek" writer Peyser
16 Common flower
19 "___ that funny?"
23 "The Sweetheart of Sigma ___"
24 Loathsome
26 Home, metaphorically
29 Baseball stat.
30 Beer barrel
31 Computer cookie, e.g.
32 Boito's Mefistofele, e.g.
34 Leave in a hurry, with "out"
36 Books that retail in large numbers
43 "Song of the Golden Calf," e.g.
44 Short garment
45 "Phooey!"
46 Earp at the O.K. Corral

Down

1 Beta preceder
2 "Am ___ the list?": 2 wds.
3 "CSI: Miami" network
4 "Princess Mononoke" genre
5 Echoic finder
6 Standard time, initially
7 Floral ring
8 Setting for TV's "Newhart"
9 Annoy persistently
11 FBI pt.
14 Base neutralizers
16 Desire analgesics, maybe
17 Dig discovery: var.
18 Beauty pageant wear
20 "Take a chair!"
21 Corners
22 Songs
24 "I get it now!" sounds
25 Kind of lily
27 "Bah!"
28 Ensnares
32 In steerage, say
33 Soothe, as fears
35 Common Market letters, once
36 Awful
37 Victorian, for one
38 "Certainly, ___!"
39 "The Joy Luck Club" author Amy
40 Pilot's announcement, briefly
41 The "R" in AARP
42 "Quiet on the ___!"

67

Across

1 Old record label
5 Certain fur
10 Film rating org.
11 Novelist Amado
12 "Hey … over here!"
13 Amount of medicine
14 Asian cuisine
16 Contingencies
17 "___ Lazy River": 2 wds.
19 Blue cartoon figure
21 Indian restaurant bread
22 Farm layer
23 ___ bit: 2 wds.
26 Soap ingredient
27 British verb ending
28 URL ender
29 "Oy ___!"
30 Capt.'s guess
31 Cost-of-living no.
32 Continental cash
34 Danger in Afghanistan, initially
35 "Man of a Thousand Faces" Chaney
36 Backside
38 Cowlike
40 Supercelebrity, like Oprah or Madonna
43 Food Network show "___ Cakes": 2 wds.
44 Attys.' degrees
45 Glacial mountain lakes
46 "I ___ Dark Stranger" (1946 movie): 2 wds.

Down

1 Band booster: abbr.
2 Defaces with rolls?: abbr.
3 View: 4 wds.
4 Curse
5 Ixtapa eye
6 "___, With Love" (1967): 2 wds.
7 Road junction with a central island: 2 wds.
8 Baker's dozen?
9 Riddle-me-___
13 Place to buy cheap goods: 2 wds.
15 More pale
17 Sch. in Paradise, Nevada
18 Brit. tax system, initially
20 Anxiety
24 "Forget it!"
25 Bunched in with
33 America, with "the"
35 Like Ricky Martin's "Vida," in song
37 Afflicts
38 Louisville Slugger, e.g.
39 Only on display, initially
41 "___ to Joy"
42 "Enemy of the State" org.

68

Across

1 Palindromic title
6 Burn
11 "Enchanted April" setting
12 Apple ___ (kitchen tool)
13 Become constricted
15 Major British tabloid, with "The"
16 Each, in scores
17 When doubled, a dance
18 Folk/rock artist DiFranco
19 Sun, to Domingo
20 Easter meat serving
21 Contact, e.g.
23 In a nasty ill-tempered manner
25 Woman, in westerns
27 Density symbol
28 Makes a sudden thrust
31 Basilica feature
34 Large, ungainly fellow
35 Priestly garb
37 Egg protector
38 "South Park" kid with a two-part head
39 The Blob, essentially
40 Bit in a horse's mouth?
41 Worthy of respect or fear
44 Dig
45 Former town employee
46 Asparagus unit
47 Flip response?

Down

1 Catholic service book
2 Adjust
3 Sock-mending tool: 2 wds.
4 ___ page (up to the minute): 2 wds.
5 Talkative birds: var.
6 Regatta competitor
7 Newspaper div.
8 Morbid fear of spiders
9 "___ Weapon"
10 Like a hunk
14 Grab (onto)
22 Become droopy
24 "Bingo!"
26 Member of a sports club
28 Scottish lords
29 Homeowner's concern
30 Grubby guy
32 Unavailable for review, as documents
33 Puts in
36 Bungle
42 Future members of a species, in biology class
43 "Is" doubled?

69

Across

1 Homer Simpson's favorite beer
5 Army ranks, initially
9 "Hamlet" fop
11 Non-native, in Hawaii
13 Chortle
14 Cancel
15 Rene's "Okay"
16 Med. land
18 Modern-day storage medium, initially
19 Düsseldorf direction
20 ___ water (it's from the faucet)
21 Freudian topic
22 Compensates
24 Had a hankering
26 Tickler of the ivories
28 Compulsive thief: abbr.
30 Marine creature
33 Composer-conductor Calloway
34 Flight coordinators, initially
36 G.I.'s address
37 Diplomat: abbr.
38 "omg thats 2 funny"
39 "Shop ___ you drop"
40 Rich kid in "Nancy"
42 ___ curiae (friends of the court)
44 Sheep fats
45 Wined and dined, perhaps
46 Blog feeds, initially
47 Massachusetts motto opener

Down

1 Computer language iteration: 2 wds.
2 Olympics chant: 2 wds.
3 Breakfast brand since 1971: 2 wds.
4 Cookie fruit
5 Wrinkly-skinned dog: 2 wds.
6 Devotee
7 Denseness
8 Gunk
10 Voucher
12 Scott of "Men in Trees"
17 Decline: 3 wds.
23 Have a bit of, as brandy
25 D.C. advisory group
27 Clueless: 3 wds.
28 Some 1980s Chryslers: 2 wds.
29 Love interest of Crosby and Hope
31 High points
32 Large meteor that explodes
35 Cat's scratcher
41 Capt.'s inferiors
43 Broadway's "Five Guys Named ___"

70

Across

1 Gem State capital
6 Yellowish-beige color
10 Prefix meaning nine
11 Boxer Ali
13 Military student
14 Fitzgerald and others
15 Ben Jonson wrote one to himself
16 Common postgrad degs.
18 Division of time
19 Yoga class need
20 2002 British Open winner
21 Hallow ending
22 "Able was I ___ saw Elba": 2 wds.
24 Baby Boom follower: 2 wds.
26 Suit material
28 Coup ___
31 Palindromic title of respect
33 New Age composer John
34 Ethel Waters' "___ Blue?": 2 wds.
36 European carrier letters
38 Secretive govt. branch
39 Managed
40 Beginning
41 ___ Francisco Bay
42 "Slow down, it's not ___": 2 wds.
44 Permanently written: 2 wds.
46 Kind of joint
47 Overplay one's part
48 Advertising sign gas
49 Wrinkled

Down

1 Turns into
2 How stunts are often done: 2 wds
3 Not fixed or known in advance
4 Catch on
5 Wonderland cake message: 2 wds.
6 Sanctified
7 Suffix with intellect
8 .txt, e.g.: 2 wds.
9 Distress signal
12 Wise-owl connector: 2 wds.
17 H.S. subject
23 Supermarket with a red oval logo, initially
25 Basketball or tennis equipment
27 Oriental
29 The Man Armand of "You Can't Have It"
30 Expressed gratitude
32 Chinese chairman
34 Composer Khachaturian
35 California county
37 Fast speech or story
43 Head honcho, initially
45 Abbr. between a first and last name, maybe

71

Across

1 Some Olympians, nowadays
5 Ancient Peruvians
10 Auto option
11 Demi ____, actress
12 Place to which one is traveling
14 Make a copy of: abbr.
15 Unshorn sheep
16 Some fraternity men, initially
17 Before, for Burns
18 Die-rolling possibility
19 Hurricane heading, initially
20 Wall panels
22 Tout's forte
23 Data processor's data
25 Balladeer Ives
28 Capers
32 Cenozoic or Paleozoic
33 Downs' opposite
34 Do the deck
35 "Who ____?" (slangy query)
36 Ball stopper
37 Penultimate Greek letter
38 Question closely
41 Dolphins' home
42 Went white
43 Paid attention: 2 wds.
44 Wooden vehicle mounted on runners

Down

1 Membrane enveloping a lung
2 Uttered in a grating voice
3 Morsel
4 In love
5 Adult insect
6 "____ to worry"
7 Originated, as a phrase
8 In the vicinity
9 Sight, hearing, etc.
10 Did some math, maybe
13 Daily publication
21 "Texas tea"
22 Baseball's Master Melvin
24 Frees from obstruction
25 Darkens
26 Astronomy Muse
27 Drum sound: hyph.
29 Pierce, in a way
30 Estimated the price of
31 Caught a glimpse of
33 Break open
39 Bird that can't fly
40 Young woman (coll)

72

Across

1 Janitor's need
4 Scarcely any
7 ___ de mer (seasickness)
10 Actress Lupino
11 Folk singer DiFranco
12 Prince ___ Khan
13 Process of becoming smaller
16 Bird of the tit family
17 Short distance runner
19 Amphitheater section
20 Alfalfa's sweetie
24 Stephen of "Still Crazy"
25 Suffix with Jacob
26 Mixed: abbr.
29 C'est ___ (that's life): 2 wds.
31 Science of improving a population by controlled breeding
33 Cause to feel shame
36 Very wealthy person
39 Off-road transport, for short
40 Bolt securer
41 Dinghy propeller
42 Mr. Flanders, on "The Simpsons"
43 Old "muscle car," briefly
44 Actress Vardalos

Down

1 Boom box abbr.
2 Prefix with meter
3 Islets of Langerhans locale
4 Breakfast fare
5 Put into law
6 Very bad
7 Sheets changer
8 Fleshy plant
9 "Unfaithful" director Adrian
14 Slender
15 Reid of "American Pie"
17 ___ Lee Corporation
18 Air Force One passenger: abbr.
21 Alteration
22 Nonclerical
23 Hydrocarbon suffixes
27 Freshwater duck
28 Throughout the time of
29 Makeshift shelter: hyph.
30 Extremity of Saturn's ring system
32 Mortar for filling crevices
33 "Diplomacy for the Next Century" author Abba
34 Small arachnid
35 Tree-lined street, shortly
37 Thor Heyerdahl craft: 2 wds.
38 Fantasy baseball stat.

73

Across

1 "Is that so!"
4 Guy
7 Armed services org.
10 Large percussion instruments
12 Ending for pistol or haban
13 Giving out
14 100 stotinki in Bulgaria
15 Elation
16 Sailor's agreement
17 "I Once Loved ___" (Scottish folk song): 2 wds.
20 Aired a second time
22 "Hawaii Five-0" actor, Daniel ___ Kim
23 Deutsch article
24 Empty boasting
30 Educ. institution
31 Big inits. in sports utility vehicles
32 Excite, as interest
35 Middle eastern currency unit
37 Big Ten inits.
38 ___ mater (brain membrane)
40 Outdoor sports chain
41 "King Lear," for one
45 A foot wide?
46 Administer, as laws
47 Prepared for the show to start
48 Barbados clock setting letters
49 N.C.A.A. football ranking system

Down

1 Volkswagen model
2 Ice: Ger.
3 German river
4 Posts
5 ___ of Cleves
6 Neighbor of Benin
7 Like some consonant sounds
8 Norse goddess of love
9 Made on a loom
11 Wrinkly dogs
17 Descriptive wd.
18 "___ note to follow soh...": 2 wds.
19 Old nuke org.
21 Med. specialty
23 Biblical suffix
25 Inst. in Nashville
26 Brewer's product: 2 wds.
27 Starter: abbr.
28 Grandma: Ger.
29 A.T.M. maker
32 Skin openings
33 "___ Dark Stranger" (1946 spy film): 3 wds.
34 "Shhh!"
35 Air current
36 Othello's betrayer
39 Caterer's collection
42 Tarzan creator's monogram
43 700, in Roman numerals
44 Positive reply

74

Across

1 Music industry assoc.
6 Spread, as lotion: 2 wds.
11 Lifted, so to speak
12 Port town on the coast of the Sea of Japan
13 Dog-___
14 Fender guitar model, briefly
15 "Healthy Aging" author: 2 wds.
17 Indiana, the ___ State
18 Pres. election mo.
19 Make brighter
23 Fop's footwear
26 Janitor's supply
27 TV watchdog
29 Sign for a packed theater, initially
30 50–50 wager: 2 wds.
33 Sacramento is its capital
36 First word of a counting rhyme
37 Florida city
38 Hightail it
39 Chipped in chips
40 Groups of actors
41 John ___ tractors

Down

1 Fishing, perhaps
2 Light open horse-drawn carriage
3 Pliable fine-grained leather
4 Old Oldsmobile
5 Footlike parts, zoologically
6 Scene of a mysterious crash in July 1947
7 Completely and without qualification
8 Adriatic port
9 Kind of hygiene
10 Filbert or cashew
16 Nintendo system
18 Presidential advisory gp.
20 Upper house of Congress: 2 wds.
21 Disney mouse
22 "Strange Magic" band letters
24 "Ash Wednesday" poet: 2 wds.
25 Americans' Cold War rivals
28 Gridiron official: abbr.
31 Desert wanderer
32 Pickling liquid
33 Anatomical cavities
34 Períodos de 52 semanas
35 Campaign staffer
36 Key in a corner, for short

75

Across

1 Hick
5 Less of a mess
11 Busy times at the I.R.S.
12 Kind of kick
13 Fighter of pirates, initially
14 Atomic trials of the past, for short: 2 wds.
15 Sharp-pointed
17 Honorary title holders
22 Conical tooth
26 Dept. of Labor arm
27 Asian palm
28 "A Doll's House" author
29 On the qui ___
30 Jostles
31 Simian
33 Impose (upon)
38 Fillet
42 River of Flanders
43 Beach atmosphere: 2 wds.
44 Nabokov heroine and others
45 Holly or Heidi of "The Hills"
46 "Promised Land" director Gus Van ___

Down

1 Singular, to Caesar
2 Gone ___ smoke (spoiled, wasted): 2 wds.
3 Act the blowhard
4 Grandson of Sarah
5 Lacking fame: hyph.
6 ___ nous
7 Enzyme suffix
8 "___ folly to be wise"
9 D.C. summer clock setting
10 ___ gestae
16 Olin of "Chocolat"
18 Former Virginia governor Chuck
19 "That ___ true!": 2 wds.
20 Strength
21 McEwan and Somerhalder
22 Spanish wine
23 "What ___" (that's robbery): 2 words
24 Actress Campbell
25 NATO member: abbr.
28 "Why should ___ you?": 2 wds.
30 "La Dolce Vita" actress
32 Aegean region
34 Hand-woven rugs
35 Letters seen in a butcher's case
36 College bigwig
37 Formerly, in olden days
38 Mil. award
39 Fair-hiring letters
40 Prohibit
41 ___ grass

76

Across

1 Hands, to Diego
6 Bad mark
11 "Haste makes waste," e.g.
12 Beginning of a conclusion
13 Thing capable of surpassing all others: hyph.
15 Concrete
16 Change the wallpaper, say
17 Place to "take the waters"
19 "___ I say more?"
21 Cousin of a mandolin
23 "You ___ kidding!"
27 Honor ___ thieves
29 Promising one
30 Analyzes a sentence
32 Type of type
33 Assistance
35 Blue shade
36 A long way off
39 "Under the Net" author Murdoch
41 Star sign
45 Cuckoo
46 Choker
47 Be of one mind
48 Claim as one's own, as land

Down

1 Big mouth
2 Big hullabaloo
3 Storyteller
4 Eye amorously
5 Accord, e.g.
6 "___ Bop" (1984 Cyndi Lauper hit)
7 Sign of sorrow
8 A chip, maybe
9 Closed, as a deal
10 "Quo Vadis?" emperor
14 Bungled, as a task
17 Fresh guy's comeuppance
18 Mountain cat
20 Org. until 1993
22 Hold sacred
24 Discharge into the air
25 Guitar part
26 Cafeteria need
28 "Holy moly!"
31 Open, as an envelope
34 "Breath of life" in Hindu religion
36 Bhutan locale
37 Long tooth
38 Chinese gelatin
40 "Pumping ___"
42 Ball raiser
43 "It's no ___!"
44 Birth certificate notation

77

Across

1 Steven ___, "Belly of the Beast" star
7 Initially, a company boss
10 Live on a host, as of parasites
11 Squarish in shape
12 Cold dressing served with fish: 2 wds.
14 Sings jazzily
15 Edmonton skater
16 Prefix with sphere
17 Spenders' binges
18 Literary monogram
19 Pelted with rocks
20 Brewery output
21 Grins
23 Fed. construction overseer
26 Glass container for laboratory use
27 Irish isle
28 They may write jingles
29 Stigmatize
30 News newbie: 2 wds.
32 Wood sorrels
33 ___ longue
34 Old video game inits.
35 Intimate meetings

Down

1 ___ table (dines): 2 wds.
2 Establishes as law
3 Letter-shaped house: hyph.
4 Arrive at: 2 wds.
5 Film speed ratings, initially
6 Photocopier option: abbr.
7 Grand ___ Dam
8 Go beyond the bounds of
9 Court documents
11 Scottish infants
13 Torpid states
17 Grab the wheel
19 Moon goddess
20 Some gang members
21 Tempt successfully
22 Fearsome snakes
23 Free
24 Least wild
25 Classical guitarist Segovia
26 Breakfast sizzler
27 Impressive display
29 1922 Physics Nobelist
31 Loan figure: abbr.

78

Across

1 Sounded off like a raven
6 Florida's Miami-___ County
10 ___ citato
11 Monthly util. bill
12 He hosted "Lifestyles of the Rich and Famous": 2 wds.
14 Banned chemical compound
15 Lowest point
16 Sits up for food
17 Collector's old French coin
20 One of the three Fates
23 Swedish automaker owned by NEVS
24 Carol of "The Pajama Game"
25 Japanese food
26 Have ___ good authority: 2 wds.
27 Very last part: 2 wds.
28 Decimal system base
29 "___ pastore" (opera by Mozart): 2 wds.
30 "Star Wars" droid Artoo-___
32 U.S.A.F. weapon
35 Mormon temple
37 Seaweed substance
38 Dirt
39 Prohibits
40 1979 peace treaty signer Anwar ___

Down

1 Army rank: abbr.
2 Book of the N.T.
3 Mary ___, author of "Precious Bane"
4 Verdi's "___ tu"
5 Actor Brian of "F/X" and "Tommy Boy"
6 Exploits
7 Kyrgyzstan's ___ Mountain
8 Cut
9 Command level: abbr.
13 Italy's ___ di Como
16 Bingo call: 2 wds.
18 "High Hopes" lyricist
19 eBay competitor
20 Gambler's marker
21 After the due date
22 Five Nations tribe
23 Black Kapital Records founder Knight
25 Some beachwear
27 Flower: Sp.
29 Brain passages
31 Abba ___ of politics
32 Battery fluid
33 ___ mater
34 Have a gathering
35 Word after pull or bar
36 Rome's ___ Pacis

79

Across

1 ___ breve
5 Associate
11 ___ & Chandon, champagne
12 Moonstruck: 2 wds.
13 Divided avenue: abbr.
14 Lose your temper: 2 wds.
15 Epithet of the mother of Romulus and Remus
16 Annoyance
17 Time in Illinois when it's noon in California: 2 wds.
19 Flat
21 Vex
24 Preschool attendee
25 "The Daughter of Time" writer Josephine
27 Bygone bird
28 Adept
29 Spirit raiser?
31 Italian town NW of Venice
32 Brass that looks like gold
36 Platte River tribe
39 One who wins by losing
40 Biggest city in the USA, initially: 2 wds.
41 Card game for two
42 Chaotic places
43 Put more bullets in
44 Boot out

Down

1 Prefix meaning "both"
2 Be lazy
3 Float in the air
4 Early in the morning: 2 wds.
5 Stressful: hyph.
6 11 hours ahead of the answer to 17-Across: 2 wds.
7 Diner orders, initially
8 ___ de plume (literary aliases)
9 ___ Office (president's place)
10 Eliot's "Adam ___"
18 Grain for horses
19 1968 hit "Harper Valley ___"
20 ___ cit.
21 Response to "This is what works for me": 3 wds.
22 Bird of myth
23 Actor Hakeem ___-Kazim of "24"
26 USN cleric, for short
30 Football coach Amos ___ Stagg
31 Prince Valiant's princess
32 Baltic feeder
33 Basmati, e.g.
34 A hearty one is square
35 Other, in Oaxaca
37 Lennon's in-laws
38 Method: abbr.

80

Across

1 The way things currently stand: 3 wds.
7 Grad. school
11 Levels
12 No longer around
13 Pet
14 Opposed to, at first?
15 Hurricane's center
16 "___ believe in yesterday": 2 wds.
18 ___ Tech
19 Computer giant, initially
20 Modern sing-along
22 Harness race pace
24 Had a hankering
25 Part of many German surnames
27 Dict. offering
28 Church official
31 Flip
34 Crew member
36 Stephen of "V for Vendetta"
37 ID-assigning org.
38 Seek damages
39 Animal's mouth
40 Publishing #
42 Indian gentlemen
44 Colorado feeder
45 Parisian palace
46 Former hair removal product
47 Group of seven

Down

1 Way up
2 Person in for the long haul
3 Impossible to get back
4 ___ Bo (Billy Blanks program)
5 "Don't worry": 2 wds.
6 Walk nonchalantly
7 Sch. in Athens or its bulldog mascot
8 Dissenter, rebel
9 Amount eaten
10 Like some threats
17 Plenty mad
21 Work without ___ (take risks): 2 wds.
23 High spots
26 "___ Island" (2008 movie starring Jodie Foster)
28 Assist in securing a loan: hyph.
29 Canine TV star
30 Gives rise to, induces
32 Navy builder
33 Carpenter's need: 2 wds.
35 Fraser of tennis
41 Rebellious Turner
43 Triangle part: abbr.

81

Across

1 Angler's quarry
5 Gather on the surface, chemically
11 Astringent
12 Carrier
13 Political matriarch: 2 wds.
15 Copy, for short
16 Canadian pop duo ___ and Sara
17 Attempts
19 Hyperbolic sine
21 Honeydew-producing aphid: 2 wds.
25 Antiquity, in antiquity
26 180 degrees from WSW
27 South American wood sorrel
28 Giants' footballer Jennings
30 Gym floor covers
31 Dined at a diner, say: 2 wds.
33 256 in Ancient Rome
36 "Ad ___ per aspera" (Kansas' state motto)
39 Woman abducted by Paris in Greek myth: 3 wds.
41 Strange fact
42 Campbell of "Scream 3"
43 Shooting iron
44 Golf pegs

Down

1 "Roseanne" star
2 ___ vera
3 Postpones
4 U.S.S.R. counter-espionage org.
5 "Honest" president
6 Gum brand with the varieties "Fire" and "Ice"
7 Least crazy
8 Wash. neighbor
9 Hester's emblem: 2 wds.
10 ___ Mawr, Pa.
14 Sends to the canvas, briefly
18 "Biography" network: 3 wds.
19 Father's talk: abbr.
20 Dockworker's org.
22 Clothing stand: 2 wds.
23 After Sept.
24 "We ___ robbed!"
26 Gnaw away at: 2 wds.
29 "I ___ on good authority": 2 wds.
30 Contraction meaning "taboo"
32 Big brute
33 Hack
34 Accra money
35 Attys.' degrees
37 Amble
38 Navy replies
40 Olive ___ (Popeye's lady)

82

Across

1 "Paging Dr. ___" (CNN show)
6 Govt. security: hyph.
11 Up ___ (cornered): 2 wds.
12 Half of an old comedy duo
13 Clairvoyants
14 "Chaplin" actress Kelly
15 Disney movie with a 2010 sequel
17 Boat propellers
18 Average guy
20 Algae bed?
22 Gen. Robt. ___: 2 wds.
24 Occurring in spring
28 Afterwards
30 Drudges
31 Not uttered
33 "Two Years Before the Mast" writer
34 Extraordinary, in Scotland
36 All the rage
37 Spot on the air?: abbr., 2 wds.
40 Old Fords, sometimes
42 Gulf of Aqaba port
44 "___ Ben Jonson" (inscription on a tomb)
47 Arcade flubs
48 Ground
49 Early ___ (no night owl)
50 Comedian Wanda of "Curb Your Enthusiasm"

Down

1 Auto-tank filler
2 Adaptable truck, for short
3 9-to-12 set
4 Dakota, once: abbr.
5 B.C. fabulist
6 ___ Sawyer
7 Crimson: 2 wds.
8 Hip bones
9 Commuter rail company, initially
10 Cow's digs
16 11th of 12: abbr.
18 "___, Joy of Man's Desiring"
19 Lena in "Havana"
21 Fiber knot
23 Tailless
25 Biblical boat: 2 wds.
26 ___ mundi
27 Aspiring atty.'s exam
29 German one
32 650 in Roman numerals
35 Relatives of the Missouria
37 Four: prefix
38 Eight, to Nero
39 "___ fair in love and war"
41 Heavy cart
43 Early role-playing game co., initially
45 A1A, I65, or 66, e.g.
46 "Huh?" sounds

83

Across

1 Winnowed-out corn husks
6 Suffer a financial loss, slangily: 2 wds.
11 Introvert
12 Battle venue
13 Gloss over, like a syllable
14 Pulverize, almost
15 Dentures: 2 wds.
17 Lemon rind
18 Too little
22 Knight and Danson
26 Bride's destination
27 West Pointer
28 Life stories, for short
29 One on the go
30 Difficult obligation
32 Skilled soprano singer
38 Cooks in an oven
39 Hackneyed
40 1983 Nicholas Gage book
41 "Seven Samurai" director Kurosawa
42 Duck feathers used in pillows
43 "Paradise Lost" figure

Down

1 Pitch indicator
2 Spanish greeting
3 Dye-yielding plant
4 U.S. government agents, briefly
5 Device for making ice cream
6 Chair designer Charles
7 Short opera songs
8 Camping shelter
9 Short distance
10 Menlo Park initials
16 Prefix with mite or minus
18 Queen of the fairies
19 Wallach of "Cinderella Liberty"
20 ___ Z: 2 wds.
21 Refined petroleum (var.)
23 Old letter (Ð)
24 Low grade
25 Orch. section
27 Winter melons
29 "Major" in Munich
31 Polite refusal: 2 wds.
32 Colombian city
33 Rubber-stamped
34 100 paisa in Bangladesh
35 The "U" in I.C.U.
36 Avis adjective
37 Alda or Greenspan
38 Spelling contest

84

Across

1 Sprayed in a way
6 Adjusts into an exact position
11 Greek poem composed of couplets
12 Man of Marseilles
13 Brit's service discharge
14 Fanatical
15 Diamond authority, for short
16 Like fans
18 Largest city in Washington
20 "Do the Right Thing" director Spike
21 Oakley and Leibovitz
22 "___ Island" (2008 movie starring Jodie Foster)
23 ___ and outs
24 "Arabian Nights" creature
25 Court helper: hyph.
27 Micromanager's concern
30 Actor McKellen
31 Salk Institute for Biological Studies site: 2 wds.
32 Great Plains tribe
34 Cassette successors, for short
35 Part of a healthy diet
36 Words on a desk box: 2 wds.
38 Reigned over
39 "Odyssey" enchantress
40 "___ of pottage" (what Esau sold his birthright for): 2 wds.
41 Broke off

Down

1 Snake-haired horror
2 Cave dwellers
3 Sociable
4 Tokyo, once
5 Argues
6 Pang
7 Crowd noise
8 Source of a fetus's food: 2 wds.
9 "8 Mile" actor
10 Marsh plants
17 Inventories of injured sports players, intially
19 Baby
22 Say ___ (turn down): 2 wds.
24 Celebrate
25 Nigerian civil war site, 1967–70
26 Element #56
27 "Camptown Races" syllable
28 Moniker for Mussolini: 2 wds.
29 Went the distance
31 Cooking fats
33 Shopping centers?
37 "Children of the Albatross" author

85

Across

1 Addition figure
4 1980s TV E.T.
7 Economic stat.
8 "Norma ___" (Sally Field film)
9 Non-Rx, initially
12 Hosp. areas for surgeons
13 Auto with a history: 2 wds.
15 Clan emblem
17 Summons from above: 2 wds.
18 Wyndham Lewis novel
19 Shopaholic's delight
20 Mint family member
24 Downy surface
25 To the extent that: 3 wds.
27 Goon's gun
29 Right a wrong
32 First word of the "Aeneid"
34 Intestinal parts
35 Olympic racers
37 Make aware
38 Necklace adornment
40 Bible translation, e.g.: abbr.
41 Founded: abbr.
42 River islet
43 Old Spanish queen
44 Apt. ad stat
45 Tiny knot of fiber

Down

1 Renata of opera fame
2 Hubbub
3 Ill-use
4 Boxing promoter Bob
5 ___ Cruces, New Mexico
6 Lawyers' charges
9 2001 George Clooney movie: 2 wds.
10 Motown's original name
11 Total loser
14 ___ Moines, Iowa
16 Units of energy
21 It's south of Eur.
22 Dumfries denial
23 Former California fort
26 Seed coat
27 Peninsula and town in Quebec
28 City on the Rhone
30 Part of H.S.H.
31 Small-time dictator
33 Contribute
36 Coal-rich German region
37 Lawyers: abbr.
39 Takeaway game

86

Across

1 Hindu garments
6 Bucks
11 Mushroom-cloud creator: abbr., 2 wds.
12 Serf
13 Do ___ situation: 2 wds.
14 Smooth over
15 1920s–50s papal name
16 100 céntimos
17 Computer key for emergencies
18 Little shaver
19 Portuguese king
20 Meat pin
22 Work without ___ (be daring): 2 wds.
23 Flat tortilla with various toppings
25 Melville tale of the South Seas
27 Indian drum: hyph
30 Film studio
31 Carpentry tool
32 So I think, online
33 Georges ___, Romanian violinist, composer, and conductor
35 Declare
36 Another time
37 Poplar tree
38 Baseball manager Joe
39 "Sunflowers" setting
40 "Someone ___ America" (1996 film)
41 Address, as a person: 2 wds.

Down

1 Urban Legends Reference Pages website
2 In jeopardy: 2 wds.
3 Make cry: 3 wds.
4 Egyptian fertility goddess
5 ___-Anne-des-Plaines, Quebec
6 Bit
7 Golf pegs
8 Instead
9 Col. Sanders feature
10 Narrow waterway
16 Trilogy's middle section: 2 wds.
18 French article
21 Seek the affection of
22 USNA rank
24 Company that owns MapQuest
25 Fatty acid salt
26 Genghis Khan, e.g.
28 Breakfast order
29 To a greater degree: 2 wds.
31 Rosacea and vulgaris
34 Be the father of
35 Incantation opener
37 Battery buys, initially

87

Across

1 Modern F/X field
4 Buffoon
7 Bouncer's checks
10 Mandela's org.
11 Myrna of "The Thin Man"
12 Big devotee
13 Multistoried adobe houses
15 Hawaiian "guitar," for short
16 Of the seashore
18 Bring excitement to, with "up"
21 Corpulent plus
22 "Ah, me!"
23 Born long ago
24 Appetizer: 2 wds.
29 Cry of disgust
30 Enlarge, as a hole
31 Governmental representative
34 Courtroom statements
35 Mount Rushmore, e.g.
37 Before: prefix
38 Element #33
42 ___ Tacs (breath mints)
43 Delicacy
44 "First off..."
45 Chatter
46 Extreme ending
47 Econ. indicator

Down

1 Pen cover
2 Serengeti grazer
3 Bar stock
4 Exhausted: 2 wds.
5 Chimney sweep's covering
6 Part of a heartbeat
7 Accustom
8 "The Sorcerer's Apprentice" composer Paul
9 Commemorative marker
14 Response to a sneeze: 2 wds.
17 Inflexible
18 ___-di-dah (pretentious)
19 United Nations agcy.
20 Alt. spelling
23 "___ Baby Baby" (Linda Ronstadt hit)
25 Frightening trance experienced while awake
26 Dog doc
27 Bowl sound
28 German river
31 Below low
32 Arabian waterwheel
33 Sweater cut: hyph.
34 Assault
36 Love, personified
39 Egg ___
40 Business off the highway
41 Much sought after mushroom

88

Across

1 Gangster's gal
5 Sepp Blatter's org.
9 Bailiwicks
11 Goes for the gold?
12 Gangster Frank, "The Enforcer"
13 Cat, in Cagliari
14 Eminent
15 "Rings ___ Fingers" (Henry Fonda film): 2 wds.
16 Holly
17 "___ la guerre"
18 Gen ___: hyph.
19 Someone ___ (not mine)
22 Dump
25 Medical care company
26 ___-jongg
28 Lat., Lith., and Ukr., once
30 Dramatic opening?
31 "___ Grows in Brooklyn": 2 wds.
33 "I ___ dream" (M. L. King Jr.): 2 wds.
34 Comes down
35 Attack ad, maybe
36 Connect with: 2 wds.
37 Manicurist's concern
38 "The Pearl of ___ Island" (Harriet Beecher Stowe novel)
39 Bygone blade

Down

1 1960s–70s TV sleuth
2 Camden Yard team
3 Mailman: 2 wds.
4 Glove material
5 Woman engaged to be married
6 Similar: 4 wds.
7 Festivals
8 Somewhat, after "of": 2 wds.
10 "___ and Nancy"
11 Tropical fruit, in short
19 Absorb, as a loss
20 Hosp. employee, perhaps
21 "___ Na Na" (1970s musical series)
23 Feels bitter about
24 Draft beer: 2 wds.
27 Croaky
28 Painter Andrea del ___
29 Flight segment
30 Ladies of the house, informally
32 "___ Beso" (1962 hit)
33 QVC rival

89

Across

1 Full of back talk
6 Igneous rock, originally
11 Host the event
12 Assumed identity
13 Elephantine
14 Division of a year
15 Bookie's lines
16 Acting Aykroyd
17 ___-Wan Kenobi ("Star Wars" role)
19 Sticky substances
23 Eddied
27 Attorneys' org.
28 Conned
29 Lingered over lunch, e.g.
30 Big load
31 Boiling blood
32 Wailer
34 Sphagnum moss
36 Bar stock
37 Cow chow
39 "Not to mention …"
43 Corsage's place
46 Six Day War hero
47 Accustom (to)
48 Dreary sound
49 Uses a keyboard
50 Amount of hair

Down

1 Utah state flower
2 In the thick of
3 Large amount
4 Electric eye, e.g.
5 At a future time
6 Cass Elliot, once
7 Beside
8 Bathtub booze
9 Spare key hider
10 ___ Wednesday
16 Relating to food intake
18 Give away
20 Four-letter word
21 Double-reed woodwind
22 Compos mentis
23 "The Flying Dutchman," e.g.
24 Silver suffix
25 Brainchild
26 Controvert
33 Bracing coastal atmosphere: 2 wds.
35 In that place
38 Beers
40 Hand-held harp
41 Drops off
42 Certain column
43 Beyond tipsy
44 "___ Given Sunday" (Al Pacino film)
45 Little Labrador
46 Banned insecticide, initially

90

Across

1. Clock div.
4. Rate at which computer data is transferred, initially
7. Word used to express disgust, slangily
10. Long ___ (way back when)
11. Suffix for chicka or campo
12. Unit of conductance
13. Group elected to govern a city
16. Abode
17. Worn out
18. Small air-breathing arthropod
21. Natural hideout
22. Horizontal fence post
24. Dutch painter Gerard ___ Borch
25. Pilgrams' ship
28. Glaswegian's cap
29. Plant of the arum family
30. Crooked
32. More spine-tingling
36. Divination deck
38. Constant
39. Lowest atmospheric layer
42. Lucy of "Charlie's Angels," 2000
43. Cookbook phrase: 2 wds.
44. Negative answers
45. Federal warning system activated by FEMA
46. 24 hours
47. 180° from WNW

Down

1. Speed of sound: 2 wds.
2. "How Can ___?" (Freddie Mercury song): 3 wds.
3. Standards
4. Friend in the 'hood
5. For each
6. Senator's possession
7. Territory ruled by an Islamic monarch
8. No one in particular
9. Marvel
14. Prying
15. Nervous twitch
19. Bistro
20. Spanish mark
23. Prospector's bonanza
25. Disease transmitted by the mosquito
26. Passionate
27. Fort ___, Texas
28. Squeal
31. Bursting balloon's sound
33. Castle of dancing
34. New money on the Continent
35. Witherspoon of "Legally Blonde"
37. Despicable sort
40. Patty Hearst's kidnap grp.
41. Foot the bill

91

Across

1 Large pill used in veterinary medicine
6 Ishmael's captain
10 Involving a single component (math)
11 Tennis's Monica
13 Rebuke angrily, lambast
15 Bruce of martial arts
16 Tic-tac-toe line
17 Reading and Short Line, in Monopoly: abbr.
18 Affirmative votes: var.
19 Middleman: abbr.
20 Novelist Rita ___ Brown
21 Juicy, gritty-textured fruit
23 Scatterbrained
25 Eskimo boat
27 Bristles
29 Author Robert ___ Butler
33 Hot dog holder
34 Lacking liquid
36 Queen of Thebes in Greek mythology
37 Certain linemen: abbr.
38 Female antelope
39 Self-centered entity
40 Stain inherited from Adam: 2 wds.
43 Wheeled cart
44 French queen
45 Glitch
46 Lowest cards in pinochle

Down

1 Canvas woven from jute
2 Cyclops' feature: 2 wds.
3 City in Southern California: 2 wds.
4 Tail: prefix
5 Church council
6 Seat of Clatsop County, Oregon
7 Billy Joel's "Tell ___ About It"
8 Security devices
9 Reveal treacherously
12 Mobutu ___ Seko of Zaire
14 Continue, doggedly: 2 wds.
22 Groove
24 Fight-ending letters
26 "Far From the ___ Crowd" (Hardy novel)
27 Buddhist scriptures
28 Banner
30 ___ wait (prepares to ambush): 2 wds.
31 Locomotive
32 Not belonging to anybody: 2 wds.
33 Expel air through pursed lips
35 Hanker (for)
41 ___ long way (last): 2 wds.
42 Hula dancer's wreath

92

Across

1 Declares
6 Chilean range
11 Relating to ecological stages
12 Street show, old style
13 Kissinger or Mancini
14 Fairy-bluebird genus
15 Long-legged, long-necked bird
16 ___ Rommel, "The Desert Fox"
17 Intentions
18 Shinzo ___, prime minister of Japan
19 Family tree word
20 1980 Tony-winning musical
23 Crybabies
26 Government bond, for short: hyph.
27 "Losing My Religion" rock group
29 Bit of numerical trivia
31 Fiery prefix
32 Like some cereals
34 Certain citrus fruits
35 Skirt style: hyph.
36 Some collars
37 Antlered animal
38 Midafternoon hour
39 Stayed in a lodge
40 Rock in Australia

Down

1 Depth charge, slangily
2 Woodland birds with speckled breasts
3 Decoration
4 Alerts
5 Leonard ___ (Roy Rogers)
6 Indy winner Luyendyk
7 Recount
8 "Blended" costar: 2 wds.
9 First word of a counting rhyme
10 Hannity and Penn
20 Leftist president Morales
21 Animal tender
22 Québec's ___ d'Orléans
24 Passionate
25 More peaceful
28 Small spore-producing plants
29 Phrase of agreement: 3 wds.
30 Bird's claw
31 Concise
33 Desideratum
34 "I ___ Song Go Out of My Heart" (Duke Ellington song): 2 wds.

93

Across

1 Femme fatale
6 Popular printing font
11 "___ Little Prayer" (Dionne Warwick hit): 3 wds.
12 "Lovergirl" singer ___ Marie
13 Theaters, slangily
14 Aggregate
15 Cave roof deposit
17 Act as a substitute: 2 wds.
18 English professor's deg.
20 Veteran: 2 wds.
24 U.K. award letters
25 Certain time zone letters
26 Oklahoma town
27 Film Dr. with an island
29 Mrs.'s counterparts, in Mexico
30 Enter forcibly
32 Earnestly religious: hyph.
36 Tough Tyler Perry character
37 Area of South Africa, KwaZulu-___
38 Astrologer Sydney
39 Late British princess
40 No longer in
41 "To recap ...": 2 wds.

Down

1 Unleashes
2 "___ really true?": 2 wds.
3 Chased: 2 wds.
4 Pupil protector
5 Twangy
6 Slanted: 3 wds.
7 Tell again
8 "___ guys like you for breakfast!": 2 wds.
9 "As I Lay Dying" father
10 ___ Vegas, Nevada
16 Permanent shutdown
18 "Pink Panther" films actor
19 Nigerian native
21 Musical solo suites
22 Nutrition stat.
23 W. hemisphere grp.
25 Payment for travel on a bus
28 Large sea ducks
29 Ankle trouble
31 Nicholson Baker story: 3 wds.
32 Portuguese explorer Vasco da ___
33 Harem rooms
34 Half of Mork's sign-off, on "Mork & Mindy"
35 Glitzy rock style
36 Kitchen floor tool

94

Across

1 Closes
6 ___ and aahs
10 Skater Harding
11 Does as instructed
13 Decoration for wounded soldiers: 2 wds.
15 Ethnic group of Vietnam
16 "Weekend Update" show, initially
17 Never, in Nuremberg
18 Crisp flat tortilla
20 Hair may hide it
21 ___'acte (break between two parts of a play)
22 Comedienne Boosler
24 With 26-Across: "Foundation's Edge" author
26 See 24-Across
29 ___ pit
33 Car tire abbr.
34 "Killing Me Softly with His Song" singer Flack
36 Mary of "Where Eagles Dare"
37 Bygone daily MTV series, informally
38 Boulogne-sur-___
39 Tiny time period
42 Accord, e.g.
43 Basil's "Captain Blood" costar
44 "You ___?"
45 Odes, sonnets, etc.

Down

1 Florida beach town, familiarly: 2 wds.
2 Sculptor Jean-Antoine ___
3 Civil ___ (riot conditions)
4 Newspaper worker: abbr.
5 Chip dip
6 "C'est magnifique!": hyph.
7 Honorary U.K. title, initially
8 "Death of a Naturalist" poet
9 Native of Damascus
12 Metric volume
14 Essays
19 Barber's job
23 #1 spot
25 Laundry job
26 Calla lilies
27 Comparatively quick
28 Marcos with a lot of shoes
30 At least: 2 wds.
31 Dictation experts, briefly
32 Not quite
35 Censor sound
40 Linked-computers acronym
41 ___ Magnon

95

Across

1 OPEC meas.
5 Little and large, e.g.: abbr.
9 Alley Oop's heartthrob
11 Chalkboard
13 Key material
14 Michelle ___, author of "Cleopatra's Daughter"
15 ___ for Lion: 2 wds.
16 G.I.'s address
18 Z preceder?: 2 wds.
19 Denver to Detroit dir.
20 Santa's shouts
21 Afghan coin
22 Interpret
24 Wealth
26 "I've no objection": 2 wds.
28 Gaming guru John
30 First James Bond movie: 2 wds.
33 Minor player
34 Mandela's org.
36 Begin to drowse off
37 Gold, in Guatemala
38 1959 Kingston Trio hit
39 Prefix with culture
40 Dropped a line
42 Mayberry's Goober and Gomer
44 Floods with light
45 Canonized person
46 Peggy and Spike
47 "Serpico" author Peter

Down

1 Big water heater
2 Cowlike
3 Completely relaxed: 4 wds.
4 Kind of camera, initially
5 Gradual absorption
6 Mideast inits.
7 Accoutrement
8 Lady Liberty, e.g.
10 Indian nanny
12 Organic compounds
17 Omen
23 In the middle of, briefly
25 Mil. officer's charge
27 Muddled: 3 wds.
28 Glower
29 Pen for livestock
31 Nine-day Catholic prayer
32 Rhapsodic poets
35 Stadium souvenirs
41 Driving need
43 Starchy food

96

Across

1 Walk loudly

6 Big party

10 "Texas Chainsaw 3D" star Raymonde

11 One of the Obama girls

12 Person who held office before

14 In the past

15 "___ man walks into a bar...": 2 wds.

16 "Blubberella" director Boll

17 Mark of perfection

18 H.S. subject

19 Sleep stage, initially

20 Flower stalk

22 Suzanne of "Three's Company"

24 Alphabet intro

26 Movable indicator on a computer screen

29 Chip's partner

33 Cortés's gold

34 Crude material

36 "Who Wants to ___ Millionaire": 2 wds.

37 Draft letters

38 Decorates with bathroom tissue, for short

39 Carrier to Stockholm, for short

40 One who sells seats: 2 wds.

43 Arboreal lizard with a throat fan

44 2:50, vis-à-vis 3:00: 2 wds.

45 Give the appearance of being

46 "My Theodosia" author Anya

Down

1 March 17 celebration, for short: 2 wds.

2 Wal-Mart rival

3 Early even score: hyph.

4 Prefix for way or west

5 Bel ___ cheese

6 Some degs.

7 Make promises to

8 Bathroom fixture

9 Muslim women's quarters

11 Poseidon, e.g.: 2 wds.

13 Person enlisted compulsorily

21 Humanities degs.

23 Club ___

25 Baby's soft shoe

26 Talk show host Bob

27 Relating to bears

28 William Kennedy novel

30 Gone

31 Shanty: hyph.

32 City on the Lehigh and Delaware rivers

35 Exams for aspiring D.A.s

41 Royal Dutch Airlines, initially

42 "Wow!"

97

Across

1. Ships' places at a wharf
7. Escaped: 2 wds.
8. Half-___ (coffee mix): abbr.
11. Visual representations in a printed publication
12. Grp. for a defensive person?
13. Lansing to Flint dir.
14. Inner part of a nut
16. Dish out
19. Agrees (with)
20. Grave marker
22. Combustible heap
23. British blue-bloods: abbr.
25. Greek goddess of discord
27. "Center" starts with one: 2 wds.
29. Passenger ship
31. "It's ___ World" (2007 drama film): 2 wds.
33. Like lemon juice
35. ___ d'Orléans
36. Brown from the sun
37. Person unlikely to be successful: hyph.
40. H.S. class
41. Spells, etc.
42. Matt ___, The Brain in "Brick"

Down

1. Noble partner
2. Providing amusement
3. Cold and wet
4. Couple
5. Listen, old style
6. Comedian Wanda of "Curb Your Enthusiasm"
7. Explorer John and others
8. Volunteer worker in a hospital: 2 wds.
9. Have ___ (drink ale): 2 wds.
10. Bogus
15. Exploit financially: 2 wds.
17. Knowledgeable about (with "in")
18. Samuel's teacher, in the Bible
21. Donkey's cousin
24. Come ___ halt: 2 wds.
25. Fill with joy
26. Costa ___
28. Veg. of the parsley family
30. Erstwhile detergent brand
32. Strange and frightening: var.
34. Refrigerate
38. Charlemagne's domain, for short
39. Tuberous plant of the Andes

98

Across

1 Flood residues
5 Singer Guthrie and street skater Eisenberg
10 Intestinal parts
11 Marcos of the Philippines
12 Former Chargers/Patriots linebacker Junior
13 "I'm impressed!": 2 wds.
14 Boston basketballer
16 "Back in the ___"
17 Highway divider
19 Brit. honor, initially
21 Hot spot
25 3-D exam
26 "___ the fields ..."
27 Suffix with Caesar
28 Crooner Frank
30 "60 Minutes" network
31 "Four Essays on Liberty" author Berlin
33 Stargazing, in college course books: abbr.
36 Sponsor of Ameritrade Park, Omaha: 2 wds.
39 Sentimental movie, to a Brit.
41 "Cogito, ___ sum": Descartes
42 Ancient: hyp.
43 Stravinsky ballet
44 Deadens
45 ___ Verde National Park

Down

1 Catchall abbr.
2 "___'s Gold" (1997 movie about a beekeeper)
3 New player's declaration: 3 wds.
4 Brown
5 "Yo te ___"
6 Adjust, in a way
7 Lawyers' degs.
8 Harem rooms
9 Baghdad's ___ City
11 Destroyed in a furnace
15 Numbskulls
18 Frightened
19 Baseball V.I.P.s
20 Man's nickname
22 Fill again, as energy in a battery
23 Apprehend
24 Come-___ (advertising ploys)
29 Cook corn, in a way: 2 wds.
32 At right angles to the keel
33 Lots, as of bills: 2 wds.
34 ___ Genesis (video game company)
35 Abound
37 Non-profit, voluntary citizens' groups, initially
38 Hawaiian coffee
40 French pronoun

99

Across

1 ___ grip (wrestling hold)
8 New Deal org.
11 Gush
12 New walker
13 "The Case of Charles Dexter Ward" author: 3 wds.
15 Flying high
16 Former unit of currency in Peru
17 "These are the times that try ___ souls" (Thomas Paine)
18 "Up" actor Ed
19 Airport abbr.
20 Cameraman's count: 2 wds.
22 Effervescent drink made from fermented cow's milk
23 Niacin or thiamine, e.g.
26 CD follower
29 Become unnavigable in winter: 2 wds.
30 Contradict
31 Crowd sound
32 Alert another car with a honk: 2 wds.
34 Journalist's scoop: 2 wds.
36 Fanciful story
37 Binds together: 2 wds.
38 Outer: prefix
39 Plastic component

Down

1 Big plan
2 Pill variety
3 Cuba or Jamaica
4 English variety
5 Prepare for a rainy day
6 Had too much, briefly
7 ___ center
8 Prefix meaning "tin"
9 Tone down
10 Garb
14 Stair part
18 Comparable (to)
20 ___ worker (non-permanent staff): abbr.
21 Movie org. with a "100 Years..." series
22 Coniferous tree of New Zealand
23 Very manly
24 Classic, as an image
25 Cups, saucers, etc.: 2 wds.
26 Lounge
27 Jogging: 3 wds.
28 "Sorry, you're not ___" (classic rejection): 2 wds.
30 Block
32 Defeat
33 Athlete's award, initially
35 Skid row woe letters

100

Across

1 Dealt (with), as a problem
6 Crack
11 Convex molding
12 Musical show
13 Restorative
14 Former little kids
15 Baby-talk characteristic
17 "Ahem" relative
18 Auspices: var.
20 "To each ___ own"
22 Blue
23 Weapon worn in a belt
27 "Das Boot" setting: hyph.
29 Hawaiian island
30 Type of fossil fuel
32 10th anniversary material
33 Bank offering, briefly
34 Pull apart
35 Luck of the Irish
38 Fertilizer component
40 Cockeyed
42 ___ of roses
45 Check endorser
46 Military tactic
47 Glove material, perhaps
48 Biblical king

Down

1 Firms: abbr.
2 Eggs, in biology
3 Tadpole
4 "The King"
5 Bucks' mates
6 "…but is it ___?"
7 Submarine zone: 2 wds.
8 Times to call, in classifieds
9 Painful plays on words
10 Assay or essay, perhaps
16 21st Greek letter
18 12th month of the Jewish civil year
19 Asia's largest desert
21 Doing nothing
23 Ado
24 Tamandua
25 Prince's "Purple ___"
26 Brain
28 Liqueur flavoring
31 Plato's "T"
34 Adjust one's laces
35 Beanies
36 Biblical birthright seller
37 ___ Terrier
39 Diaper woe
41 Itsy-bitsy
43 Back then
44 Brave opponent

101

Across

1 City on the Skunk River
5 Belong: 2 wds.
10 Scholastic sports grp.
11 "West Side Story" girl
12 Seasoned sailors
13 European language
14 Winter Palace resident
16 Sushi fish
17 Hearth residue
19 Family head
21 Ad ___ committee
22 Pollution-fighting org.
23 Decryption org.
26 Before, before
27 Deighton or Dykstra
28 Jimjams, initially
29 Grown-up boys
30 One ___ million: 2 wds.
31 Ms. West
32 N.Y.C.-based international org.: 2 wds.
34 Time, in Torino
35 Wide shoe spec
36 Mediator's asset
38 Put emphasis on
40 French river
43 CivPro students: 2 wds.
44 Fossil fuel
45 Verb with thou
46 First numbers

Down

1 Colony crawler
2 Major record label letters
3 Like some Pagan religious traditions: hyph.
4 Disrespect
5 Baby ___ (1984 baboon heart recipient)
6 Against a thing, legally: 2 wds.
7 Efficiency evaluation procedure, ___ study: hyph.
8 Slanted type: abbr.
9 Bert Bobbsey's twin sister
13 Corn Flakes rival: hyph.
15 2001 French film starring Audrey Tautou
17 Attention-getting cough
18 Irritated
20 Tomorrow, in Spain
24 Stage-door symbol
25 On the ocean
33 Back parts of human feet
35 Europe's largest volcano
37 Designer Chanel
38 Fifth musical scale note
39 Grounded fast flier, initially
41 Bill accompanier, initially
42 Golf champ Ernie

102

Across

1 Hello, in Hawaii
6 Greek letter
9 Thesaurus compiler
10 "It Had to Be ___"
11 Arctic animal: 2 wds.
13 Soap, e.g.
14 Works in the garden
16 Popeye's creator E. C. ___
20 Deaf person's communication letters
21 Spartan
23 Small town on a railroad: hyph.
25 Excluded: 2 wds.
26 Try hard to win
27 Lightened (up)
28 Uses crosshairs
29 Whodunit awards
32 Staff
35 Card with a letter on it
36 Seaport on northern Honshu Island, Japan
37 Lawn base
38 Teen soap opera series: 2 wds.

Down

1 Dadaist Jean
2 Indiscreet talk: 2 wds.
3 Looks at lustfully
4 Get the word
5 "The Bell of ___" (Longfellow)
6 Small holes for threading a lace through
7 ___ T: 2 wds.
8 Sound-related prefix

12 Sturdy hunting dog with big ears
14 "The Phenom" star Ethan
15 Comic actress Tessie
17 Become aware of: 3 wds.
18 E. M. Forster's "___ With a View"
19 Bank takebacks, briefly
21 In disagreement: 2 wds.
22 Inuit woman's all-purpose knife
24 Operated a rudder

28 Golfer Palmer, to pals
30 Bearded animal
31 Emblem of life
32 Pops
33 Prefix with logical
34 Anita Brookner's "Hotel du ___"

103

Across

1 Ammonia derivative
6 Buds
10 Chief Justice after Marshall
11 Pope after John X: 2 wds.
12 "___ as I can see": 2 wds.
13 ABC sitcom
14 One way to get up a mountain: 2 wds.
16 Big: abbr.
17 100 yrs.
18 1997 U.S. Open champ
19 "___ on a Grecian Urn"
20 "Grazie ___!" (Italian for "Thank God!")
22 ___ blood (having murderous intentions): 2 wds.
24 Sawbuck: hyph.
26 "Turandot" and "Tosca"
28 "Eureka!" shouts
31 "___ Kapital" (Karl Marx)
32 E-mail ID, in short
34 Big music publisher, initially
35 "Either she goes, ___ go": 2 wds.
36 Put down
38 Greek valley where games were held
40 See 37-Down
41 Zoo dart, for short
42 Ball game
43 1952 Winter Olympics city
44 Grab the wheel

Down

1 Lake ___, source of the Mississippi
2 Disguised
3 Immeasurably small
4 "Hud" Oscar winner
5 High nest: var.
6 ___ canto
7 Risky attempt to do something: 4 wds.
8 Exaggerate
9 Parton or Sinatra, e.g.
11 Eases: 2 wds.
15 One of the Bobbseys
21 "___ the fields we go"
23 Keats's "Ode ___ Nightingale": 2 wds.
25 Computerized system for trading in securities, initially
26 Tooth: prefix
27 Kitchen gadgets
29 Punish with an arbitrary penalty
30 Crablike mover
33 Snatches
37 With 40-Across, Tripping Daisy song of 1995: 2 wds.
39 "Achtung Baby" co-producer Brian

104

Across

1 Some German cars, initially
5 Big name in pizza
11 Comedian Lew
12 Prevailed: 2 wds.
13 Some nest eggs, initially
14 Prefix with phosphate
15 1/100th div.
16 ___ polloi
17 "Call Me Maybe" singer Carly ___ Jepsen
18 "The Hermit" author Eugène
21 Aloof
22 Chorus voice
26 Destroys
27 Moves, in real estate jargon
28 A chorus line
29 Spicy condiment
30 Makes more orderly
32 Danger in Afghanistan, initially
35 Calypso kin
36 Capital of Ga.
38 Treeless plain
40 Plant with fleshy leaves
41 "___ Lonesome Tonight?": 2 wds.
42 Real estate ad abbr.
43 Clean, as a floor: 2 wds.
44 Low islands

Down

1 Radar image
2 Forgiving
3 "Does it matter?": 3 wds.
4 12th graders: abbr.
5 Rushing sound
6 Kind of acid
7 Director ___ Lee
8 Big laugh
9 ___ temperature: 2 wds.
10 Oklahoma tribe member
16 Dame Myra
19 Sheer, smooth fabric
20 Built round?
21 "___ et labora" (pray and work)
23 "M*A*S*H" actor: 2 wds.
24 Sorry tale: 2 wds.
25 F.I.C.A. benefit
27 Pro ___
29 Kind of call: 2 wds.
31 City in Finland
32 "___ what you did!": 2 wds.
33 Peut-___ (maybe, in Paris)
34 Bug repellent brand
37 Moon vehicles, initially
39 Poe's "The Narrative of Arthur Gordon ___"
40 "20/20" network

105

Across

1 Mrs. Eisenhower
6 Domesticated
10 Beautify
11 As a companion
13 Pack again, as groceries
14 Cuplike spoon
15 551, in Ancient Rome
16 ___ system, initially
18 Aachen article
19 Suffix with tutor or torrent
20 Settle
22 Earth, in Berlin
24 Layer
25 Winged
27 Medicinal plant
28 Blanched
29 Defeated
30 Going round and round: 3 wds.
32 Spaniard's "that"
35 Kernel's home
36 Crack pilot
37 "Losing My Religion" band
38 "I Once Loved ___" (Scottish folk song): 2 wds.
40 Cups and saucers
42 Casino maximum
43 Clamorous
44 "The Lion King" lion
45 Sealy competitor

Down

1 ___ Gras
2 ___ Rogers St. Johns
3 Gulf Coast city: 2 wds.
4 Investment program, for short
5 Duelist's warning: 2 wds.
6 Daedalus' nephew
7 Dinner ___ carte: 2 wds.
8 Decorator's showcase, sometimes: 2 wds.
9 Animate
12 Biological groups
17 Honey maker
21 Traditional dance from Tahiti
23 Hwy. abbrs.
25 At the tip
26 Substance found on sheep's wool
27 Native New Yorkers
29 Pen name
31 Fettuccelle, e.g.
33 French legislature
34 Actress Kate of "Dynasty"
39 The "S" in R.S.V.P.
41 Maximilian's realm, initially

106

Across

1. Diminish, with "off"
6. Another name for a crook
11. Radiations of light
12. Source of sesame seed
13. Cleans up, in a way
14. C ancestor, initially
15. Sue Grafton's "___ for Lawless": 2 wds.
16. It's cold, regardless of climate
18. UN working conditions agcy.
19. "___ (I Will Understand)" (Britney Spears song)
21. ATM need
22. Copy: abbr.
23. ___ legs (dog's pair)
24. Commerce free of tariffs, quotas, etc.: 2 wds.
27. Atomic particle
28. Letters that mean "you'll get paid back"
29. South American wood sorrel
30. Produce and discharge eggs
34. University conferral, initially
35. Barbie's beau
36. Game with matchsticks
37. Banana oil, e.g.
39. Wild Asian dog
41. Divine huntress
42. Duck down
43. Jazz instruments, for short
44. Carmen Agra ___, "14 Cows for America" author

Down

1. Asian weight units
2. Part of a TV transmission
3. Geometrical solid
4. Graze, e.g.
5. What's left
6. "___ Road" (Beatles album)
7. Actress Thompson of "Caroline in the City"
8. Flat
9. Oily liquid used in synthetic dyes
10. Minute part
17. Type of audience
20. Costar of TV's "How to Marry a Millionaire"
23. Considerable winnings, informally
24. Reddish purple
25. Driver's duty: 2 wds.
26. Having a smooth, curved surface
27. Motorized cycles
30. Cajun veggies
31. Cell terminal
32. Like some floors
33. Coarse stuff for manicurists
38. Ending for benz or ethyl
40. Get going

107

Across

1 Bristol-Myers roll-on brand
4 Father's Day gift giver, perhaps
7 Do the math, maybe
10 Ironically funny
11 "___, four, six, eight, who do we appreciate?"
12 Flowers around your neck, in Hawaii
13 Military combat vehicles: 2 wds.
16 Sheets of rock that have been moved more than 2 kms.
17 "Lucky Jim" author
18 Doughy
19 Garlic bulb
20 Gull
22 Datebook abbr.
23 Lawyer's gp.
26 Bladed paddle
27 D.C. setting, initially
28 ___ Aviv
29 "Surfer," so to speak
31 Accounts
33 Smash hits, slangily
37 Chemical compound
38 Blood carrier
39 It makes the air feel colder: 2 wds.
41 Barbarous one
42 "Have some"
43 Action film staple
44 Bloke
45 "___ you being served?"
46 Caribbean, e.g.

Down

1 Swahili sahib
2 Hanging tapestry
3 Insect larva
4 Testing one's powers of endurance
5 Has a mortgage
6 Affirmative indication
7 Apple pie order?: 3 wds.
8 Originates from
9 Analyze
14 Gazette page: hyph.
15 ___ Ripken, Jr. (baseball great)
19 Cogitate
21 Dance bit
23 Kind of case
24 Great grip
25 Teaming up (with)
30 DOD recruiting program
32 Angular joint
34 Embryo's successor
35 Preserved, in a way
36 Its flag has two green stars
38 On the horizon, perhaps
40 Actress Salonga or Thompson

108

Across

1 Wander away: 2 wds.
8 Sunny state, for short
11 Morse who sang "Cow-Cow Boogie": 2 wds.
12 Daughter of Theia
13 Start of the year: 3 wds.
15 Free-trade org. based in Jakarta
16 ___ Janeiro: 2 wds.
17 It doesn't gather on rolling stones
18 Attic
19 Ending for persist or consist
20 Look over again, as an article
21 High hideaway
22 Jerks
24 Basketball game figure with a whistle, for short
27 Swimmer Michael
28 Mobutu ___ Seko of Zaire
29 Sought help from: 2 wds.
30 Lift, old-style
31 Blasé
33 502, in Herod's day
34 "The ___ Madonna" (Raphael painting)
35 Suffix with rep or rev
36 Santa Claus in the 2003 comedy "Elf": 2 wds.

Down

1 Label again, as a computer file
2 Nels of "Little House on the Prairie"
3 Where Astros and Angels play: 2 wds.
4 Central American Indians
5 Black cat, e.g.
6 J.F.K. overseer
7 Sporty Italian cars
8 Hat worn by Indiana Jones
9 Charged with ammunition
10 To date: 2 wds.
14 "No ___ Bob!"
18 Bacteria
20 Answer
21 Finnish architect Alvar ___
22 Country singer Twain
23 Plan tentatively, with "in"
24 Control, as costs: 2 wds.
25 Ancient Semite
26 Bird seed holder
27 Victorian, maybe
28 Alphabetizes, e.g.
30 "___ Rebel" (1962 hit): 2 wds.
32 El ___ (1961 Charlton Heston role)

109

Across

1 Bookbinder's tools
5 "All You Need ___" (Morrissey song): 2 wds.
9 Synthesizer pioneer
10 Archeological find
12 Italy's shape
13 Burnt ___ (Crayola color)
14 Masthead contents, briefly
15 "Can ___ least sit down?": 2 wds.
16 "Am ___ trouble?": 2 wds.
17 Riddle-me-___ (rhyme)
18 "___: Miami" (CBS hit)
19 Agent's take
20 Slithering creatures
22 Big name in gasoline
23 Some bagel toppers
25 Kind of ball, in baseball
27 Aqua ___, acid used in rocket fuels
30 Cleaning cloth
31 "Are you a man ___ mouse?": 2 wds.
32 "___ you joking?"
33 "Can ___ now?": 2 wds.
34 Pistol, in old gangster movies
35 Craggy prominence
36 Runs off (with)
38 French film
39 Take in again
40 Masked animal, for short
41 Abbreviated moments
42 Rest stop, once

Down

1 Fossil resins
2 Stiff
3 Casual and relaxed: 4 wds.
4 ___ Pepper
5 Last Supper query: 3 wds.
6 "___ Believes In Me" (Kenny Rogers hit)
7 Appearance of a ghost
8 Golfer Els and comic Kovacs
11 Copenhageners
13 Leaves used to make filé
15 "Italian" treats
21 "Mad Men" account executive Cosgrove
22 "And I Love ___"
24 Castle defense
25 Pipe type
26 Golf coups
28 Affixable, in a way: hyph.
29 Collected
31 Double-S curves
37 Chest muscle
38 LXVII, tripled

110

Across

1 Turkish general
5 Wuss
10 Used
11 Clearly surprised
12 Of the blood
13 Arrive, as darkness: 2 wds.
14 Sad feelings of gloom and inadequacy
16 Arduous journeys
17 Austrian peaks
20 Son of Erebus and night
24 Gun, as an engine
25 Practice, as a trade
26 "America's Most Wanted" letters
27 Rogue
29 "Absolutely!"
30 Try to achieve, as a goal: 2 wds.
32 One who works his own land: 2 wds.
37 Charitable organization, e.g.
38 Spacious
39 Ellington and Wellington
40 High nest: var.
41 Clandestine meeting
42 Live wire, so to speak

Down

1 "Hard ___!" (captain's cry)
2 Hobbling gait
3 Playing card suit
4 "Inferiority complex" theorist
5 It opens many doors
6 Certain discriminator
7 Brussels-based alliance, initially
8 "Music for Life" magazine
9 Appetite
10 High degree, initially
15 Block up: 2 wds.
17 "Mustache Hat" artist Jean
18 Fragrant garland
19 Cable material, initially
21 "Green Eggs and ___"
22 Just make, with "out"
23 Bolted
25 Complain
28 Concurs
29 Rocky ravine
31 Propelled a boat
32 Forbidding
33 Black
34 "Encore!"
35 Arabic for "commander"
36 Bread for a pastrami sandwich
37 Environmental no-no, initially

111

Across

1 "Cool" amount of money
4 "Enemy of the State" org.
7 ___ blond
10 ___ de coeur
11 Sandwich, initially
12 Narc's org.
13 Spring outlook: 2 wds.
16 Cote de ___ (French entree)
17 Seat in stone for several persons
18 Debaucher
20 Wading birds
23 Letter-shaped construction piece: hyph.
27 Indonesian island
28 "___ sorry!" (apology): 3 wds.
29 Kitchen item: abbr.
30 Green
31 Japanese immigrant
33 Singer Twain
36 Supervisors, briefly
40 Kid's summertime employment: 2 wds.
42 Max Fleischer's Olive
43 "___ Largo"
44 Berne's river
45 Accelerator pedal
46 "Boo-o-o!"
47 Online feed, initially

Down

1 1205, to Nero
2 "Dies ___"
3 Singer McCann
4 Compass point, initially
5 Precipitates icily
6 Inability to co-ordinate voluntary movements
7 What Ritalin treats, for short
8 Ball handler?
9 ___-kiri
14 Italian dictator
15 Italian verse form: 2 wds.
19 Aviation prefix
20 "Give ___ try!": 2 wds.
21 Marcel Marceau character
22 Rascal
24 ASCAP rival
25 Nile nipper
26 Kind of deer
28 Chemical suffix
30 Conventions
32 Kitchen features
33 Bad air
34 Georgetown athlete
35 Punchers
37 "Battle Maximus" band
38 Cell messenger letters
39 Lat., Lith., and Ukr., once
41 River of France and Belgium

112

Across

1 "___ Alone"
5 Act the siren
10 Sharp
12 Aromas
13 "Who's there?" reply: 2 wds.
14 Seed again
15 Back muscle, familiarly
16 Definite article
18 In the capacity of
19 Certain sets, for short
20 Suffix with cash
21 "Anchors Aweigh" gp.
22 "Amazing!"
24 Dolores Haze's story
26 Director's domain: 2 wds.
28 Hard to understand
30 ___ scale
33 Fellow, in British slang
34 Volkswagen hatchback
36 "Fantasia" unit
37 Celestial altar
38 Mil. aide
39 "First of all…"
40 Court org. 1920–75: 2 wds.
42 Bit of a merry refrain: hyph.
44 Conductor Solti
45 Enough, in French
46 "It's a Wonderful Life" role
47 Eye affliction

Down

1 "___ The Chief": 2 wds.
2 Book size
3 2001 Anjelica Huston miniseries, with "The": 3 wds.
4 Harvard deg.
5 Bullfighters
6 Ethnic group of Vietnam
7 Region of Nicaragua: 2 wds.
8 French analytical chemist (1754–1826)
9 Member of a Bantu people
11 Bhutan beast
17 Protective headgear
23 Game played with pegs: hyph.
25 "Solaris" author Stanislaw
27 Traveler's need
28 Model railroad scale: hyph.
29 Cruise officer
31 Don of the Eagles
32 Blackguard
35 Greek letter, or a tiny bit
41 Prefix meaning "three"
43 Online feed, initially

113

Across

1 Biology lab bacteria: 2 wds.
6 Sugar source
11 Make a dash toward: 2 wds.
12 Bull, of sorts
13 Queen's place: 3 wds.
15 "Song of the South" song syllables
16 Essen exclamation
17 "Empedocles on ___" (Matthew Arnold poem)
19 Community studies deg.
22 Agatha Christie detective
25 "I ___ Dark Stranger" (1946 movie): 2 wds.
26 Sudden feeling of fear: 2 wds.
28 Brake part
29 Ducts
30 Big ___
31 Agenda unit
32 Kamoze of reggae
33 Apple seeds
37 Coins often given away: 2 wds.
41 Flyer that extended its name in 1997
42 "Beat it!"
43 Explosive experiment: abbr., 2 wds.
44 "Who's there?" response: 3 wds.

Down

1 "Das Rheingold" goddess
2 Gave prompts to
3 A while ago
4 War of 1812 locale: 2 wds.
5 City in Japan
6 Big drawer?
7 Wife of Esau
8 Muslim saint or holy man
9 Calculator feature, initially
10 Aliens, for short
14 Wonderful
18 It has a lot of chapters, initially
19 Unable to hear
20 Denomination
21 ___ Fifth Avenue
22 Ltr. addenda
23 Hawaiian island
24 "___ out?" (poker query): 2 wds.
25 British Parliament outrage of 1765
27 First word, often
31 Dead to the world
32 Pupil's place
34 Calvary inscription: inits.
35 Major golf tourneys, initially
36 Hauler on the highway
37 Bright light
38 "Hey, you!"
39 Dental org.
40 Chinese philosopher Chu ___

114

Across

1 Superman wears one
5 Forced out
11 Biblical pronoun
12 Causing a sensation as of things crawling on the skin
13 Say once more: 2 wds.
15 ___ Palmas
16 ___ Mitchell, Double G on "Game Shakers"
17 Presley's label, initially
18 Brandy, whiskey, etc.
20 Astronaut Grissom
21 Burro's relative
22 Blowgun missile
23 Recipe amts.
26 Baseball Hall-of-Famer, ___ Stengel
27 The "W" of kWh
28 Bud
29 ___ Proudfoot (cousin of Bilbo Baggins)
30 Aims for, with a gun: 2 wds.
34 Fish propeller
35 W.W. II vessel, briefly
36 Nationals grp.
37 Uplifting enlightenment
40 Tell, as a story
41 Tax pros, briefly
42 Agree: 2 wds.
43 Nota ___

Down

1 "Save" shortcut on a PC: abbr., 2 wds.
2 Tons: 2 wds.
3 Brand of cola
4 Shoe box marking
5 Groups of eight
6 Mountain range from the Arctic to the Caspian Sea
7 Pc. of the whole
8 Riot control substance: 2 wds.
9 Gastronome
10 Family line
14 "___ Before Dying": 2 wds.
19 Awestruck
22 "Over" follower in the first line of "The Caissons Go Rolling Along"
23 They're sold for the price of one, slangily
24 Inadvisable plan: 2 wds.
25 In a hard or unsympathetic manner
26 Magna ___
28 Sign after Aquarius
30 Top-___ (golf ball brand)
31 Long-billed wading bird
32 Take out ___ (borrow money): 2 wds.
33 Past, present or future
38 Wray of "King Kong"
39 Elvis' motto, initially

115

Across

1 Serpentine letter
4 Latest craze
7 Stephen of "The Crying Game"
8 Lawyer's org.
9 12th graders: abbr.
12 Cut loose: 2 wds.
14 Tea, in Toulouse
15 Race of Norse gods
16 "High School Musical" star Zac
18 Abound (with)
19 Jenny "The Swedish Nightingale"
20 Priest's vestment
21 Peacenik's slogan: 2 wds.
24 Attribute
26 Edge: 2 wds.
28 Suffix with expert
31 Doctors who check out head colds, for short
32 Blues great ___ James
33 "Paradise Lost" figure
35 Hearts
36 Shag rug made in Sweden
37 Hard to get
39 Vintner's prefix
40 ___ amis
41 102, to a Roman
42 Mozart opera "Die Entfuehrung ___ dem Serail"
43 Egg layer

Down

1 Mistakes in a book
2 Marine creature: 2 wds.
3 Spanish port and resort: 2 wds.
4 Carnival
5 Blood-typing letters
6 Watch feature, perhaps
9 Hit the jackpot: 3 wds.
10 Avignon's river
11 Mails
13 Canyon feature
17 Bungle
21 Sgt., for one
22 Sch. in Tulsa, Oklahoma
23 ___-picking (petty)
25 Zaire's Mobutu ___ Seko
26 Prefix with surgery or transmitter
27 Deli specification: 2 wds.
29 Wonder who sang "Superstition"
30 Introduce gently: 2 wds.
32 Greek goddess of dawn
34 "Champagne Tony" of golf
35 Use a bad word
38 Romania's currency

116

Across

1 Sculptress Hepworth
8 Down Under bird
11 Not lubricated
12 ___ gestae
13 Grinling ___, sculptor (1648–1721)
14 Beer keg outlet
15 Grassy area
16 Naval rank: abbr.
17 Hamburg's river
20 Central point
23 Slap on
24 Before, in poetry
25 Band of eight
27 Certain sorority woman
31 Money in Moldova
33 Attractive device
34 Disastrous
36 Burrow
37 Boor
38 Bluejacket
40 Low noise
41 Tower on a mosque
45 Alicia of "Falcon Crest"
46 Characterized by strong feelings
47 Shot that moves across a landscape
48 Spoiled: 2 wds.

Down

1 Harmful microorganism
2 DiFranco of pop
3 Plunder
4 Areas where Protestant fundamentalism is widespread: 2 wds.
5 Cosmetic additive
6 File menu option
7 Pop-ups, often: abbr.
8 Romain de Tirtoff's, familiarly
9 Destined
10 Door-to-door service, initially
17 Nigerian language
18 Fond du ___, Wisc.
19 On the other hand
21 Make upset
22 Speed at which a population declines: 2 wds.
26 Afternoon break
28 Experienced
29 Chum
30 Mighty Joe Young, for one
32 Last month
34 Catalog of animals
35 He concocts campaigns
37 Bloke
39 Unsigned, as a poem
41 Ryan of "When Harry Met Sally"
42 "Spare" body part
43 Eddie's "Green Acres" costar
44 "Hazel" cartoonist Key

117

Across

1 Brazilian dance
6 Ladybug features
11 Some doctoral exams
12 Sal who co-starred with James Dean
13 Herbaceous plants
14 Actress Tatum
15 Pizza ___
16 Negating word
18 "There ___ way out": 2 wds.
19 Cigar remains
20 Educ. institution
21 Japanese computer giant, initially
22 Cooperative unit
24 Discussion
26 Small pouch
28 Battering device
29 "Lights! Camera! ___!"
32 Female deer
35 Buck's partner
36 Bass ___
38 Pastoral place
39 ___ Jones Industrial Average
40 Color in Japan's flag
41 Mil. titles
42 RBI or ERA, e.g.
44 "The Frugal Gourmet" Jeff
46 Clipped
47 School, in French
48 "Entertaining Mr. Sloane" playwright
49 Like notebook paper

Down

1 "Who cares?": 2 wds.
2 Get excited
3 Billionaire with her own "Living" magazine: 2 wds.
4 Deli request, initially
5 Grps.
6 Put out a fire, one way
7 ATM code
8 Very long odds of winning: 4 wds.
9 Saucers, cups, et al: 2 wds.
10 Comfort in distress
17 Need to tidy things away all the time, say: inits.
23 Printemps month
25 "Phooey!"
27 Become less refined
29 Augments: 2 wds.
30 "The Dukes of Hazzard" garage owner
31 Nationals grp.
33 Rub the wrong way
34 Having gaps or spaces
37 1950s Ford flop
43 General on some Chinese menus
45 Long distance letters, once

118

Across

1 Musical symbols that indicate pitch
6 It has Old and New Testaments
11 Caste member
12 Theater employee
13 Imprison, confine
15 Stephen of "Michael Collins"
16 Suffix with Caesar
17 Sends to the canvas, briefly
18 Some batteries, initially
19 Grp. directed by Marin Alsop
20 Egyptian boy king, shortly
21 Anne of ___, Henry VIII's fourth wife
23 In ___ (as found)
24 Reverses a dele
26 Olympic hurdler Jones
29 Wandered
33 "Kate & Allie" actress Meyers
34 Letters in a help wanted ad
35 "We ___ Not Alone" (1939 film)
36 Nien Rebellion general
37 Sweet treatment, briefly
38 L.A. to Las Vegas dir.
39 Having a merciful disposition
42 January, to Julio
43 Analyze syntactically
44 Undersides
45 Blue-gray shade

Down

1 Former French president Jacques
2 In a straight line of descent
3 Protect, in a way
4 Pharmaceutical watchdog grp.
5 Certainty: 2 wds.
6 It's good in Mexico
7 Mideast land: abbr.
8 Loving devotion to a Hindu deity
9 Make known: 2 wds.
10 "Are you" in Spain: 2 wds.
14 Oven-cooked stew
22 Poverty-fighting grp.
23 Govt. agency that has your number
25 Boot reinforcements
26 Jewish potato pancakes
27 Duke in "Twelfth Night"
28 "Say You, Say Me" singer Richie
30 Mystical chant
31 1908 Chemistry Nobelist Rutherford
32 Role in TV's "Hunter": 2 wds.
34 Community spirit
40 "Forgot About ___" (1999 rap song)
41 State capital of North Carolina: abbr.

119

Across

1 Hindu holy man
6 Baby bringer
11 Native Canadians
12 At full gallop
13 Ghana's capital
14 Popular mints
15 Asian language
16 Creature with a beard
18 Channel through shoals
19 Fay's role in "King Kong"
20 Ages
21 Hail, to Caesar
22 Pro follower
24 More labyrinthine
26 Skilled craftsman
28 Call
30 Terrific, in slang
33 It goes before E except after C: 2 wds.
34 Hi-___ graphics
36 New England state sch.
37 Big container
38 Like workers on a pension: abbr.
39 Little bit, as of brandy
40 Discontinue
42 Ban legally
44 Put away
45 The ones I'm holding
46 Winter forecast
47 Rip up

Down

1 Graduated
2 Secret stuff
3 Rid of harmful substances
4 Feminine pronoun
5 Web site hit count
6 Ornamental sunken panels in a ceiling
7 Gorilla, e.g.
8 Shopper who looks at for items at low prices: 2 wds.
9 Organ stop
10 One in bed
17 Party favorite
23 Chair part
25 Get with a laser gun
27 Rushing flow
28 Rémoulade and Lyonnaise
29 Imaginary
31 Songlike
32 Placed at an angle
35 Undoes, as an edit
41 Match, as a bet
43 "Quiet, please!"

120

Across

1 Sugar ___
6 Pianist Rubinstein
11 "___ its course": 2 wds.
12 Excelled
13 Safari sight
14 Gibbs of country music
15 College in New Rochelle, New York
16 One of helium's two
17 Cable channel that shows old films, initially
18 A doz. doz.
19 Motor suffix, commercially
20 "___ in St. Louis" (1944 Garland film): 2 wds.
22 Sesame, coconut and peanut
23 Those hurt, as by crime
25 Gardner and others
27 Puts (inside)
30 "Buck Rogers" actor Gerard
31 "Hath ___ sister?" (Shakespeare): 2 wds.
32 French seasoning
33 "Speaking machine" developer
35 Very, pretentiously: 2 wds.
36 Approaches
37 Take ___ breath: 2 wds.
38 Richard of "Ocean's 11"
39 Brawl
40 Swedish seaport on the Baltic
41 Gets bare on top

Down

1 Singer Makeba
2 In: 2 wds.
3 Hal Foster's comics hero: 2 wds.
4 "Sweater Girl" Turner
5 "Another Green World" composer
6 Nolan Ryan, notably
7 Stat start
8 Like some cats
9 Open, in a way
10 Spanish queens
16 Little Leaguer, e.g.
18 Big inits. in sports utility vehicles
21 "___ the season to be jolly"
22 Fed. fiscal agency
24 "___ Believer": 2 wds.
25 Service group
26 Some tapes
28 Remove the pits from
29 Math class calculations
31 Battled a blaze, perhaps
34 Mex. miss
35 Ancient theaters
37 Diplomat: abbr.

121

Across

1 Ceiling
4 "The Little Red Book" writer
7 Auction signal
10 Respectful Turkish title
11 Babysitter's handful
12 Molybdenite, e.g.
13 Tchotchke
15 "___-Tac-Dough" (1970s–80s game show)
16 Consumer Reports employee
17 ___ lily
18 Encouraging word
19 Slanted kind of type
21 Penetrating
22 Spanish percussion instrument
26 Make permanent: 2 wds.
27 Circa
28 Puts in
32 "J'accuse" author Emile
33 Sketch from the beginning
35 "___ calls?"
36 Without a stalk, in botany
37 "Dirty" tattletale
38 Battery size letters
39 Antiquity, in antiquity
40 "Do you get it?"
41 Australian runner
42 Blonde's secret, maybe

Down

1 Malicious
2 Correspond
3 Indian coin
4 Emcee's need
5 Social ideal: 2 wds.
6 Choose (with "for")
7 Short letter
8 Beginnings
9 Steep in hot water
14 ___ power
17 Astute
20 2,000 pounds
22 Haloes
23 Priest's helper
24 Gull-like bird
25 Element in a "Wizard of Oz" character's name
26 Pianist Berman and Agent "Swifty"
28 "Inc." spots?
29 Preserved, in a way
30 Waste time
31 Nobel, for one
34 Abraham's grandson
36 Ed.'s request

122

Across

1 Univ., sometimes
5 Got together
11 Check information
12 Treat badly: hyph.
13 And others, for short: 2 wds.
14 Score
15 Easily-irritated person
17 Hair-raising
18 Atlas page
21 Cover
23 Kind of change or talk
25 They come in a pack: abbr.
26 Chill
27 Page of some wall calendars
29 ___ donna
30 Dash widths
31 Of the eye
33 Hot pepper used in Mexican cooking
36 Breathing space in a line of verse
39 ___ and terminer
40 Keeps after
41 Act as usher
42 Trap: var.
43 Dangerous biters

Down

1 October 15, for example
2 Alliance acronym
3 Aries and Taurus, e.g.: 2 wds.
4 Put on
5 Kind of box
6 Irving Berlin classic
7 "Mush!" shouter's vehicle
8 Juliet, to Romeo
9 Approx.
10 "L.A. Law" actress Susan
16 Dupes
18 Transducers used to detect and measure light: 2 wds.
19 Graduate of a school, casually
20 "Not guilty," e.g.
21 Company patronized by Wile E. Coyote
22 Baum's was a coward
24 Plant with tulip-like flowers
28 Buys up
29 Elementary school group, for short
32 Shallow pool
33 May follower
34 Lowest high tide
35 Biscuit bits
36 Greek letter after phi
37 Proterozoic, for instance
38 Arithmetic result

123

Across

1 Bear, in a fairy tale
5 Wild and crazy
11 Individualists?
12 Botanical ring
13 Sore spots
14 Author Rushdie
15 Pakistani language
16 Big banger, initially
17 Marine flier
19 Out, in a way
23 Life's work
25 Bone-dry
26 Biblical craft
27 Medicinal amt.
29 Heavyweight boxer "Two ___" Tony Galento
30 Pseudologized
32 Slap the cuffs on
34 Christmas trio
35 Any of the Griffins on "Family Guy," e.g.
36 Big time
38 Laundry batch
41 One who has an effect
44 Similar to
45 Fitting measurement
46 Pennsylvanian city known as "The Gem City"
47 Livestock buildings
48 Split apart

Down

1 Andean nation
2 Jelly ingredient
3 Small barrel for explosives: 2 wds.
4 Give one's word
5 High-ranking naval officers: 3 wds.
6 Flaherty's "Man of ___"
7 River formations
8 Dot-___ (internet company)
9 Made like, in cookery: 2 wds.
10 Go for the gold?
18 Badminton barrier
20 Bane of one's existence: 2 wds.
21 "Aeneid" figure
22 1978 WSMVP, Bucky
23 Not all bent out of shape
24 "Mi chiamano Mimi," e.g.
28 Country club figure
31 Vin of movies
33 ___ coaster
37 Down-to-earth
39 Blood-related
40 Feat
41 Alliance that includes Kazakhstan, Kyrgyzstan, etc.
42 Aardvark's morsel
43 It's a free country, familiarly

124

Across

1 PC key
4 ___ Angelico
7 Cultural org.
8 Cartoon canine
9 General found on some Chinese menus
12 India neighbor, briefly
13 Spectacles
15 Alpine feature
17 ___ different tune (change one's mind): 2 wds.
18 1968 Chemistry Nobelist Onsager
19 Words before "uproar" or "instant": 2 wds.
20 Slip-on shoes: hyph.
24 Savings accrual: abbr.
25 "Surprised by Joy" autobiographer: 2 wds.
27 Leftist president Morales
29 To the extent that: 3 wds.
32 Neighbor of Swed.
34 Battering wind
35 Like some currents
37 Some clock sounds
38 Raise up
40 "The Jungle Book" snake
41 Computer file format, initially
42 Court figs.
43 "Slippery" tree
44 "Six-pack" on the stomach: abbr.
45 2–2 or 3–3, for instance

Down

1 Records
2 Eye with intent: 2 wds.
3 Device used in some interviews: 2 wds.
4 At no cost
5 King, in Cádiz
6 Hydrocarbon suffixes
9 Item needed at Wimbledon: 2 wds.
10 "Contact" author Carl
11 Praying figure
14 Home video game console
16 An oz. has six
21 French pronoun
22 Classic opener
23 Common personal ad letters
26 "Othello" antagonist
27 Try to win, as a contest
28 "Behold!"
30 Acid neutralizer
31 "___ Street" (famous kids' show)
33 Uncompressed audio format
36 Russian car make
37 ___ Trueheart of "Dick Tracy"
39 Computer key

125

Across

1 Melodramatic cry
5 Jefferson was one
10 Italian goodbyes
12 "So what else ___?": 2 wds.
13 Like "Lost" episodes
14 Brazilian palm
15 General on a Chinese menu
16 Heartbeat record, for short
18 Suffix with cash
19 BBC rival
20 Airport abbr.
21 Dolores ___ Rio
22 Italian "thing"
24 Flip-chart homes
26 Drop sharply
28 Largest volcano in Europe: abbr., 2 wds.
30 "Breakfast for Dinner" eatery
33 "You've got mail" ISP
34 Takeoff and landing overseers, initially
36 "A Theory of Semiotics" author
37 Currency unit of the U.S.: abbr.
38 Little, in Scotland
39 Club headed by the Bakkers, initially
40 Japanese dog
42 ___ Walton League (conservation group)
44 Salvaging aid
45 "___ Doone" (1869 novel)
46 1973 #1 Rolling Stones hit
47 Just about makes, with "out"

Down

1 ___ acid
2 Misinforms: 2 wds.
3 TV executive producer: 2 wds.
4 "___ gather": 2 wds.
5 Chart
6 Double curve
7 Kind of home run where the batter needs to run quickly: 3 wds.
8 Conger: 2 wds.
9 Rotates rapidly
11 "Did You Ever ___ Lassie?": 2 wds.
17 Incinerate
23 Key abbr.
25 Six, to Italians
27 Out of it
28 "___ March hare" (irate): 3 wds.
29 Assumed: 2 wds.
31 Gas number
32 Lively Bohemian dances
35 Cover, as a room
41 "___-Pan" (1966 novel)
43 "Avatar" actress Saldana

129

126

Across

1 Dock
6 "Deathtrap" star Christopher
11 Noted blind mathematician
12 Bay window
13 Small terrestrial lizard
14 Blasé
15 Think again!
17 Esoteric
18 City on the Yamuna River
20 Burdened with, as debt
24 Big bang producer, for short
25 Kind of approval letters
26 "___ pales in Heaven the morning star": Lowell
27 Breakfast cereal
29 Harpoon, e.g.
30 Family name on "Full House"
32 Developing rapidly
36 Indivisible unit
37 Tighten, maybe
38 Old port on the Tiber
39 Long oar at the stern of a boat
40 Fake, fraudulent: var.
41 Abates

Down

1 Become threadbare
2 More than large
3 Menu option: 3 wds.
4 Clinging fish
5 Parisian's coin, once
6 Deciduous flowering tree
7 Like many shorelines
8 Cork's country, in Gaelic
9 Dogleg
10 Former word for former days
16 Canned fish
18 24-hour bank feature, briefly
19 African animal
21 Loose material, dust
22 "The ___ of Good Feelings"
23 Lincoln's state, for short
25 14th June: 2 wds.
28 Back problem
29 "What fools these mortals be" writer
31 Like Eric the Red
32 "Poppycock!"
33 "___us a son..."
34 Christie's "Death on the ___"
35 Sets
36 Finish, with "up"

127

Across

1 City bombed in the Gulf War
6 Houses, in Spain
11 "Rings ___ Fingers" (Henry Fonda film): 2 wds.
12 44th President
13 "A Confederacy of Dunces" author
14 Out: 2 wds.
15 Caribbean city: 2 wds.
17 Military camp (Fr.)
18 Appropriately named fruit
20 Foolishness
25 Nine, in Spanish
27 City and county in Texas
28 Be pleasing (to)
30 Cover the upper surface (a room)
31 Prefix with comic
33 "Poetry Man" singer
38 Good, in Guadalajara
39 Bread spread
40 Weekdays, initially
41 Filmdom's Mr. Chips
42 ___ the opinion (thought): 2 wds.
43 Relating to

Down

1 Not just one
2 Indonesian buffalo
3 Moved with a spade
4 Not absolute
5 "Gladiator" setting
6 Yield
7 Hunt's "___ Ben Adhem"
8 Letters identifying a combination of voices (music)
9 "___ Psycho" (song by Midwest rapper Tech N9ne): 3 wds.
10 ___ Clemente
16 Bee: prefix
18 One, in France
19 Portable firearm
21 Cut
22 Confrontational: hyph.
23 102, in Roman numerals
24 Big initials in fashion
26 Die down: 2 wds.
29 Battle of Atlanta soldier
32 ___ book (be literate): 2 wds.
33 "I ___ Spell on You" (Jay Hawkins song): 2 wds.
34 Chops
35 Knowledgeable of
36 Slave in "The Good Earth"
37 1984–88 skating gold medalist
38 German automaker known by three initials

128

Across

1 Foot lever
6 Lawn plant
11 Sheriff Lobo portrayer Claude
12 "We're Off ___ the Wizard": 2 wds.
13 Country singer Carter
14 Decaf. coffee brand
15 New York baseball team
17 Partner of gloom
18 "You are" in Spain
20 Neighbor of Syr.
22 Was in session
23 Encourages: 2 wds.
27 Lunchtime for some: 2 wds.
29 Fred's dancing sister
30 Able to be attached: hyph.
32 "___ note to follow soh…": 2 wds.
33 Sony handheld device, initially
34 Pessimist's word
35 Ballet bend
38 Top guns
40 Roof projections
42 Analysis of an ore
45 Cowboy's lasso
46 Paycheck booster
47 Shoreline swoopers
48 "I need ___!": 2 wds.

Down

1 Note taker's need
2 Supplement, with "out"
3 Width of a circle
4 Burrell and Bancroft
5 Future atty.'s exam
6 Sporty cars, briefly
7 Foundation of a rail track
8 Spanish donkey
9 Zaire's Mobuto Sese ___
10 Tailor's line
16 Camera type, briefly
18 Those, to Juan
19 Go on and on
21 First governor of Alaska
23 Baseball referees, for short
24 Haile ___, emperor of Ethiopia
25 ___ Soule, TV animation voice of Batman from 1968 to 1984
26 Free of clutter
28 Capital of French Polynesia
31 ___-Locka, Florida
34 French equivalent of the Oscar
35 French father
36 Hideaway
37 John, in Moscow
39 "Flashdance… What a Feeling" singer Irene
41 Carrier to Copenhagen, initially
43 Brayer
44 Even so

129

Across

1 Self-satisfied
5 Hit hard
10 Tropical paradise on Maui
11 Language of Sri Lanka
12 Comedian Samberg
13 Had a grumble about
14 Fade away
15 Before, old-style
16 Summer on the Riviera
17 Corn unit
18 Solemn promise
19 Coll. dorm bigwigs
20 Having a grand view
22 Depositor's holding: abbr.
23 Playing marble
25 Sweater eater
27 Hullabaloo
30 "The Fallen" director Taub
31 Apt. feature in ads
32 Powerful stuff, initially
33 "McHale's Navy" actor Conway
34 Born in France
35 O.T. book, for short
36 Playing card suit
38 Blind as ___: 2 wds.
39 Lay to rest
40 ___ Romeo (Italian auto)
41 Martin or McQueen
42 Country dance

Down

1 Sunglasses
2 Lunatic
3 Regard (something) as less important than it really is
4 Writer Talese
5 Scatter about
6 It follows Avril
7 Very small or gradual
8 Cravat pin: var., 2 wds.
9 First-born
13 Certain items of food
15 1960s singer Sands
21 Greatest possible
22 Pick a target
24 Gospel writer
25 Singer Johnny
26 Set straight
28 Lacking in security
29 Relating to a nation
31 Between, in Bordeaux
37 Gun an engine
38 Solothurn's river

130

Across

1 Boldness
6 "Casino" actor Joe
11 Argument settler, often
12 Grayish
13 Beanery, in slang: 2 wds.
15 Delight
16 American Beauty, e.g.
17 Metric meas.
19 Harvard rival
21 Botanist Gray et al.
23 Greet the villain: 2 wds.
27 Irritates
29 "Cómo ___?"
30 Street warning: 2 wds.
32 Other, in Oaxaca
33 "It's you! What a surprise!": 2 wds.
35 Guys
36 Counterfeit: abbr.
39 Course on insects, for short
41 Substitute
45 Digit on a "Magic" ball
46 Food Network celeb ___ de Laurentiis
47 3s, in cards
48 Big name in printers

Down

1 Bill amt.
2 TV adjustment: abbr.
3 Monocle
4 Airline to Israel: 2 wds.
5 Nurse Ratched's creator Ken
6 Faux ___
7 Starbucks order
8 "Beat it!"
9 Corp. heads
10 Rest stop, once
14 "Awright!"
17 "CSI" actress Helgenberger
18 Aoki of the PGA
20 Fib
22 Mottled
24 Caribbean getaway: 2 wds.
25 Alpine stream
26 General ___ Chicken (Chinese menu dish)
28 Fifth note in a musical scale
31 "That was close!"
34 Years old: 2 wds.
36 "A likely story!": 2 wds.
37 Former prime minister born "Mabovich"
38 "Bus Stop" playwright
40 Fall preceder
42 Shaker ___, O.
43 Tokyo, once
44 Campaigned

131

Across

1 Old-fashioned
8 "Miss Being Mrs." singer Lynn
9 FDR predecessor
12 Lower than low
13 Celestial altar
14 Bag of chips, maybe
15 "You're getting on my ___!"
17 "The Wind in the Willows" character
19 Suffix with dirt or draft
20 Code-breaking grp.
21 Core
24 Failed to include: 2 wds.
26 Government grant
28 "___ du lieber!"
31 Aoki of the PGA
32 Column foundation piece
34 Islamic leader
37 Deception
38 The Magic, on scoreboards
39 Encourage
41 Penn. neighbor
42 Decide mutually: 2 wds.
43 Sammy of baseball fame

Down

1 Support org. formed in 1951: hyph.
2 Machines resembling human beings
3 Fortune-tellers' needs: 2 wds.
4 Politically correct pronoun: 2 wds.
5 Cash cache letters
6 Make ___ adventure: 2 wds.
7 Racer Yarborough
9 "No idea": 3 wds.
10 Dimin.'s musical opposite
11 Undue speed
16 André ___, Dutch violinist and conductor
18 Mortgage adjustment, for short
22 Avg.
23 Some beans
25 Class for foreigners, for short
26 "The Goodbye Girl" writer
27 Charging too much interest
29 Humidor item
30 Strong types: hyph.
33 Not one's cup ___: 2 wds.
35 Literary olios
36 Science fiction's ___ Award
40 B.&O. et al.

132

Across

1 Under the covers, perhaps
5 English race place
10 White, as in fear
11 "Purlie" star Moore
12 "After that …"
13 Displace
14 Blue hue
16 "What's the ___?"
17 Contracted
19 "Naughty you!"
21 Be human, perhaps
22 Drain, as someone's energy
23 Amount in a Brylcreem slogan
26 "Fantasy Island" prop
27 Altdorf's canton
28 Delighted sound
29 Disney dwarf
30 Biology class, initially
31 Khan, e.g.
32 Shout of approval
34 Debtor's ink color, traditionally
35 Despite, in odes
36 Coordinate: abbr.
38 Blood pumps
40 Bounce, as from a bar
43 Nitrogen compound
44 Engravers' equipment
45 Bender
46 "___ lively!"

Down

1 Clever
2 "___ humbug!" (Scrooge's shout)
3 Instrument of execution: 2 wds.
4 Contradict
5 Band box, shortly
6 Antitoxin
7 Limited TV system: hyph.
8 Instrument featured in "Peter and the Wolf"
9 Permanent body art, casually
13 Remove the yoke from
15 Cinch
17 Money: Ger.
18 ___ balls (chocolate covered treats)
20 Abode that's abuzz
24 Choice: hyph.
25 Niven's "Casino Royale" role
33 Attila's crew
35 Non-permanent employee, shortly
37 Indicates "yes"
38 "Rumor ___ it…"
39 Shirt with artwork, maybe
41 "___ you later!"
42 80 minims: abbr.

133

Across

1 Police rank: abbr.
5 How some music is sold: 2 wds.
10 Biting tool
12 "It's only ___!": 2 wds.
13 Data processor's data
14 Hartebeests
15 "___ where it hurts!": 2 wds.
17 Nighttime wear, for short
18 Thor Heyerdahl craft: 2 wds.
20 First-year cadet
22 Brief detail
24 Ready for slaughter
27 Acapulco assents: 2 wds.
29 Daughter of Ball and Arnaz
30 Like some cows
32 Certain cameras: inits.
33 ___ pocus
35 Comic's shriek
36 Letters after the price of a used car
38 African virus
40 C-E-G chord, e.g.
42 1991 Nicholson Baker book about his fascination with John Updike: 3 wds.
45 Greek goddess of chance
46 Wing (prefix)
47 Early year: 2 wds.
48 Eastern titles

Down

1 "Is ___?": 2 wds.
2 Sine qua ___
3 1982 movie starring Meryl Streep: 2 wds.
4 Spitting sound, in comics
5 Breakfast food
6 Aid group, often: initials.
7 Shag spiffer-upper: 2 wds.
8 Key of Bach's Brandenburg Concerto no. 5: abbr., 2 wds.
9 Meeting: abbr.
11 URL starter
16 "The Lord of the Rings" figure
18 Blog feeds, initially
19 Pacific capital
21 A/C stat.
23 Former nightclub owner
25 Cork's country
26 Carrel
28 Pulled out
31 Do a voice-over
34 Early course
36 "Beetle Bailey" barker
37 Welsh word in a Pennsylvania college name
39 Back muscles, for short
41 "Bingo!"
43 Soft & ___ (Gillette brand)
44 Greek island

134

Across

1 ___ Pie Island (artist commune on the Thames)
4 Computer button
7 Educ. group
10 Extinct flightless bird
11 Edible wood sorrel
12 Directional word
13 Not impeded by too many objects
16 Melodious
17 Née followers: 2 wds.
22 "For sale by ___"
23 Debonair
24 Bit
25 1970 Jagger film "___ Kelly"
26 Bay window
29 Appealing
31 Make counter-accusations
33 Rings
34 Deep perception of a situation
39 Pablo Picasso's field
40 Centimeter-gram-second unit
41 Many a Wall St. Journal subscriber
42 Functioned as
43 Attorney F. ___ Bailey
44 "Babe: ___ in the City" (1998 sequel)

Down

1 Bird whose meat is eaten by Australians
2 Age
3 Fond du ___, Wisc.
4 Band member on the road
5 Be part of the cast of: 2 wds.
6 They're waved in concert halls
7 Obsessive desire to set fire to things
8 Boot part
9 "Then what?"
14 Put on board, as cargo
15 Biblical brother
17 Engine
18 Cognizant
19 Certain signs
20 Javelin, e.g.
21 Bulrush, e.g.
27 Marine bird
28 Door frame part
29 Green fodder used as animal feed
30 Condo, e.g.
32 Black-and-white diving bird
34 Cat's foot
35 Historian's time
36 Dennis Mitchell or Bart Simpson
37 Geisha's girder
38 Hound

135

Across

1 Eyeballs
5 Baby bouncers
10 French rake?
11 The ___ State (Connecticut nickname)
13 Magician's word
15 Money for the server
16 Party time, maybe
17 Order between "ready" and "fire"
18 Guarantee
20 Beluga yield
21 Break
23 Beer drinker's stomach
24 Steam bath
27 Became an issue
29 "King Kong" babe
30 Averse: var.
32 ___ Alamos, N.M.
33 Unemotional
37 Pride or wrath, e.g.
38 Mail place, initially
39 "Blastoff!" preceder
40 Artifact that belongs to another time
43 Scratches left by a glacier on rocks
44 Black and white cookie
45 Granite-colored
46 Dampens

Down

1 Be bombastic
2 Early bird
3 After-dinner sounds
4 Hemingway book "The Old Man and the ___"
5 Scoundrels
6 Art subject
7 H, to Homer
8 Trade stoppage
9 Grave
12 Reproductive cell
14 Some like it hot
19 Coffee maker
22 Arm art, maybe
24 Mexican restaurant condiments
25 Consecrates with oil
26 Disentangle
28 Character used in density
31 Fish hawk
34 France's longest river
35 Hawaii's location, in atlases
36 Audition tapes, briefly
38 Steps leading down to a river in Asia
41 "The Good Shepherd" org.
42 Immediately

136

Across

1 Real heel
4 First ___ kit
7 Mouth: prefix
8 Show set in many cities initially
9 Jamaican export
12 Pacino and Gore
13 Acute intestinal infection
15 Drops of sadness
17 "___ do" (turndown): 2 wds.
18 She played Gretchen on "Benson"
19 Superior: hyph.
20 Scaly limbless reptile
24 Great deal
25 Morally correct
27 Father's Day gift, often
29 Make a sly verbal attack: 2 wds.
32 "Take a Chance ___"
   (Abba song): 2 wds.
34 Pinnacle
35 Power for old trains
37 Playful aquatic animal
38 Brazilian monetary unit
40 Monthly business magazine
41 Height: abbr.
42 Taylor or Hurley
43 Lode contents
44 It often follows you
45 Ending with exter or inter

Down

1 Raccoons' cousins
2 One-time "What's My Line?" panelist Francis
3 Lack of concensus
4 Bkprs.' records
5 Language name suffix
6 "Tank Full of Blues" singer
9 Memory
10 Heavens: prefix
11 "The Absinthe Drinker" painter
14 Mauna ___, Hawaii
16 Fully absorbed
21 Hesitant sounds
22 "Delta of Venus" writer
23 Former cable co.
26 Get ___ on the back (be praised): 2 wds.
27 Puccini opera
28 Big name in computers
30 Sun god of Ancient Egypt: hyph.
31 Toyota model
33 Consume
36 ___ fide (law)
37 Seep
39 Man, to Caesar

137

Across

1 Benefits
6 They go with the flow
11 Bluebird genus
12 Leaning
13 Not so nice
14 Sealy competitor
15 Summit
16 League: abbr.
18 Chatter
19 Actor Wallach
20 Your, in Roma
21 Collection agcy.
22 Pro follower
24 ___ Van Huong, Vietnamese Prime Minister: 1965
26 Elite U.S. Navy squad
28 Money substitute
31 Skid around
33 Move, in real estate slang
34 Tooth-doctors' org.
36 IV units
38 Dot follower
39 Martial arts promo. co.
40 Modern F/X field
41 Eggs, in biology
42 Like Eric the Red
44 Waxed, old style
46 Corp. official
47 Actor Murphy of "Trading Places"
48 Small paving stones
49 They're rigged

Down

1 Related females
2 Ring of color
3 "This is just between you and me!": 4 wds.
4 Break off
5 Verb for thou
6 East Indian sailors
7 Absorbed, as a cost
8 Sir Richard Branson started it: 2 wds.
9 Church part
10 Random guesses
17 Away from the office
23 "Is that ___?"
25 Like a lot of the entries in this puzzle: abbr.
27 Triumph
29 "That was excellent!": 3 wds.
30 Hair salon stock
32 Arrhythmia detector, briefly
34 Some female relatives
35 Prior to, in dialect
37 Command to an attack dog: 2 wds.
43 Didn't straphang
45 Writer LeShan

138

Across

1 One-___ (freak events)
5 Frozen spike
11 Bank deposit?
12 Lament
13 Deanna ___, Marina Sirtis's "Star Trek" role
14 ___ pentameter (kind of verse)
15 Strong black coffee
17 66, e.g.: abbr.
18 Appraises brazenly: 2 wds.
22 Accumulates, with "up"
24 Jackson 5 member
25 "___ Theme" ("Doctor Zhivago" song)
26 "The Faerie Queene" division
27 Lone Star State sch.
28 Narrow gorge with a stream running through it
29 "Let's Explore Diabetes with Owls" humorist David
31 Loafer designation
33 Automobile components: 2 wds.
35 Prompt
38 "So ___": 2 wds.
39 Leg wrap for soldiers
40 "Brokeback Mountain" heroine
41 More gloomy
42 Troughs for washing ores

Down

1 Blender brand
2 Ace: hyph.
3 Like some rabbits: hyph.
4 Cooking instruction
5 Wading birds
6 Knock off
7 Enduring
8 Corn core
9 "Love Story" composer Francis
10 Abbr. at the bottom of a letter
16 Antlered Alaskan animals
19 Complimentary close
20 When: 3 wds.
21 "___ bad!"
23 Power to learn
25 Light units: abbr.
26 Either horn of a crescent moon
28 Beam
30 Hindu queen
32 "Cómo ___?"
34 As blind as ___: 2 wds.
35 "World of Warcraft," e.g.
36 Part of E.U.: abbr.
37 1959 hit for The Kingston Trio

139

Across

1 "___ Adventures in Wonderland"
7 Bangkok native
11 Disperse: 2 wds.
12 Bribes
13 Rigid bracelet
14 Held back
15 Don't waste
16 "Save" shortcut on a PC: abbr., 2 wds.
17 Cedar Rapids college
19 Genetic letters
21 Former name of the cable network Versus, initially
22 Disentangle
26 Honorary law degree, initially
27 CAT scan relative
28 Make a move
29 Chinese religion
31 Measure of conductance
32 Top of the glass
34 Ability tested by Zener cards, initially
35 Clean up, in a way
38 Suppositions
40 "Free Willy" creature
41 Gourmet's sense
44 Come into view
45 Connect, as peripherals: hyph.
46 Clothing designer Taylor and TV newswoman Curry
47 Nerds

Down

1 Mil. jet locale
2 When doubled, a Teletubby
3 Insinuation
4 Gear parts
5 Noted blind mathematician
6 ___-Foy, Que.
7 Syllables of reproach: 2 wds.
8 Field worker
9 Freezer or blender, e.g.: abbr.
10 Adherents: suffix
16 "Would you allow me...?": 2 wds.
17 .45 maker
18 ___ podrida
20 1920s Olympics star from Finland
23 Junior, to Senior
24 Folk singer Phil
25 Car roof feature: hyph.
27 Amt. you don't expect to pay
30 Support group?: hyph.
33 Cat's cry
35 Gaucho's weapon
36 "Dianetics" author Hubbard: 2 wds.
37 Coll. major
39 A lot of ice
41 College prof.'s degree
42 Bath
43 Some dance records, for short

140

Across

1 Carved figure
7 Heroic tale
11 Capital of Eritrea
12 Chloracne cause, initially
13 Grossman and Campbell
14 Brewer's kiln
15 Bit of rain
16 Fabric shop purchase
18 Square dance group, e.g.
20 Shape
24 Sports artist LeRoy
26 Get a conversation going: 3 wds.
28 Try to locate
29 Blank, as a "tabula"
30 County seat of Telfair County, Georgia
31 Radial, e.g.
32 Barbara, to friends
36 Darth's daughter
38 Call used to attract attention: hyph.
40 Like a bump on ___: 2 wds.
41 Sign up, as for a class
42 Corny product
43 Alternative to a paper clip

Down

1 Beach blanket?
2 Ivan the Terrible, for one
3 "Here ___, there..." ("Old MacDonald" lyric): 2 wds.
4 Pound (down)
5 Spoon-bender Geller
6 Good-looking: 4 wds.
7 More athletic
8 Dean's domain
9 "Pygmalion" writer's monogram
10 Halifax clock setting: inits.
17 Banda ___ (Sumatran city)
19 Tic-___ (candies)
20 Some ball-carriers: abbr.
21 City near Provo
22 Response
23 Wedlock
25 Grant-giving org.
27 Dodge Aries, e.g.: hyph.
32 When doubled, a South Pacific island
33 "Just ___, skip and jump": 2 wds.
34 ___ weevil
35 It's under a foot
36 Napkin's place
37 "Don't Bring Me Down" grp.
39 Canadian province: abbr.

141

Across

1 Ad-supported online video service
5 "Li'l Abner" cartoonist: 2 wds.
11 Balin and Claire
12 Finds a new purpose for
13 Author of "The Martian Chronicles": 2 wds.
15 Skillful, competent
16 "What I think is…," initially
17 Grp. for Cardinals and Panthers
18 Deputized: 2 wds.
20 "How stupid of me!"
21 My, in Marseilles
22 Blood pigment
23 Cassettes
26 Felt concern or interest
27 Astronaut Shepard
28 Six, to Italians
29 ___ Tin Tin
30 Subterranean cell for prisoners
34 "Luck ___ Lady Tonight": 2 wds.
35 Room coolers, for short
36 ___-cone (fair cooler)
37 Not worried
40 Looked after: 2 wds.
41 ___ de soie (silk cloth)
42 Warming device
43 Small land masses: abbr.

Down

1 Takes on
2 Not fitting
3 Bring a ship to rest: 2 wds.
4 Initially a mouse port
5 A Musketeer
6 ___ a wild goose chase: 2 wds.
7 Baby bear
8 In pieces
9 Scent
10 Excited
14 Carnival attractions
19 Foreboding sign
22 Reagan Secretary of State
23 Cap similar to a fez: var.
24 Property recipient
25 Nostrum
26 Odorize by burning
28 Assistance
30 "The Divine Comedy" writer
31 Old laborers
32 Actress Tatum
33 Knotty spot
38 Minn. neighbor
39 Oldest technological univ. in America

142

Across

1 Broken-off branch
5 Conundrum
10 Dull hurt
11 In an ominous way
12 Pahlavi, e.g.
13 Ancient Roman magistrate
14 Dreadful
16 Fond du ___, Wisconsin
17 Joust weapon
21 Construction site sight
23 Ever ready
24 Blitzed
25 J.F.K. watchdog
26 Seaweed gelatins
29 Employs a stiletto
31 Excessive enthusiasm
32 Go public with
33 Take unawares
37 Small
40 Nonpareil: hyph.
41 Paid the penalty
42 Two-way
43 Euphemistic expletives
44 Catch a glimpse of

Down

1 Accessory for Miss America
2 Canyon effect
3 Flamboyant deceiver
4 1943 conference site
5 Rice dish made with saffron
6 Big test
7 Enjoy the Alps, perhaps
8 Connecting pipe
9 Monte Carlo ingredient
11 Apply gently
15 Dry ___ (it makes "smoke" in theater productions)
18 Wicked
19 Complain
20 Fraternity letters
21 Quahog or geoduck, e.g.
22 Baltic port
27 Getting up
28 Pan-fries
29 Dupe
30 Philippic
34 Valentine's Day color
35 Go ballistic
36 Hard to hold
37 Hip home
38 When a plane is due in, shortly
39 Freight weight

143

Across

1 Aniseed-flavored aperitif
7 Toy gun insert
10 Bow (to)
11 Near Eastern honorific
12 Urban acceptability: abbr., 2 wds.
14 Scoundrels: hyph.
15 Columnist Bombeck
16 Bo Diddley hit: 3 wds.
20 Oily liquid used in synthetic dyes
21 Will
25 Haviland Thin Mints manufacturer
26 Carryall: 2 wds.
28 Mellow
29 Rate of speed
33 Unique
35 Judo, e.g.: 2 wds.
37 Pal, to Pierre
38 Store, as corn
39 Gullible guy
40 Pad holders

Down

1 No longer in use
2 Cast member
3 "Get out of my sight!"
4 "Irons in the Fire" singer ___ Marie
5 Picked out of a lineup, briefly
6 Becomes established: 2 wds.
7 Lot event: 2 wds.
8 Biographical bit
9 S.O.S scouring ___
13 On the way
17 Recording device, briefly
18 Mandela's org.
19 Classical or conservative prefix
20 Even though
21 MA and PA, e.g.
22 ___-ha (uproar)
23 Law enforcement and tax collection agency, initially
24 Proceeds without restraint: 2 wds.
27 Lennox and Clark
29 Throb
30 Actor Delon
31 ___ Ponti, who produced "Doctor Zhivago"
32 Some Art Deco works
34 "Queer as Folk" actor Robert
35 Pas' partners
36 G.P.'s org.

144

Across

1 Beds for babies
6 Pipe problem
10 Wilkes-___, Pennsylvania
11 Disorient
13 Comics page feature
14 Intensely bright (color)
15 Let out
17 Look after
18 Mischievous type
20 Intention
22 Prefix with liberal or conservative
23 Bread basket bun
25 Pliant
27 Expect eagerly
29 Mature person
32 Dick Francis book "Dead ___"
34 District
35 Peg for drivers
37 It's not me
39 Dine
40 Winglike
42 Difficult burden
44 Leg bone
46 Nearby
49 Titan made to support the heavens
50 Emasculate
51 Slim swimmers
52 Weights used in China and East Asia

Down

1 Good buddies use them, initially
2 Deserter
3 Unique
4 Lip of a hat
5 Brown-tinted photo
6 John, for short
7 Blue-pencil
8 Given to running risks
9 "Dean" costar Kevin
12 Taro corm or plant
16 Frank McCourt memoir
18 One of the Gershwins
19 Do some yard work
21 Extinct flightless bird of New Zealand
24 Made-up story
26 Rx org.
28 Have a go
30 Michele ___, Rachel of "Glee"
31 Make lace
33 As well
35 "Farewell": hyph.
36 Cream of the crop
38 In its original form, as a movie
41 Iranian currency
43 Forearm bone
45 Dumbhead
47 ___ volatile (smelling salts)
48 Navy rank: abbr.

145

Across

1 Broods
6 Drinker's accident
11 Laissez-___
12 Like lions
13 When some have brunch: 2 wds.
14 "A Lesson From ___" (play)
15 Big name in food service
16 Go ballistic
17 Country singer Travis
19 Atlas plates
22 Show to the door: 2 wds.
26 Little battery size, initially
27 Est., once
28 Fatal disease of cattle, initially
29 Blue book filler
31 Carbonated quaff
32 Mikhail's spouse
34 West Point newbie
36 ___ apso (dog)
40 Caribbean cruise stop
41 "The Farnsworth Invention" playwright Sorkin
42 Script sentences
43 Muscle
44 Vichyssoise vegetables
45 Chip dip

Down

1 Advanced drama degrees, initially
2 Like Cheerios
3 Absolute worst, slangily
4 Builds
5 Casa dweller
6 More stylish
7 Gourmet's sense
8 Knowing, as a secret: 2 wds.
9 Internet writing system with unconventional spelling
10 Mormons, initially
18 Japanese immigrant
19 Go to the ___ (contend mightily)
20 Dental org.
21 "N'est ce ___?"
23 Letters after the price of a used car
24 Certain currency, initially
25 Brew "for two"
27 Marine food fish: 2 wds.
30 "Jeopardy!" host
31 1943 Bogart film
33 Big pieces, as of meat or marble
34 ___-dieu
35 Crescent
37 Asian sea
38 Farm females
39 "___ and the King of Siam"
40 Every last one

146

Across

1 All at the same time: 2 wds.
7 Triumphant cry
10 Angel of the highest order
11 It goes with neither
12 Mime groups
14 Place for P.E.
15 Bolivian president Morales
16 Need to repeatedly do things, initially
17 "When Your Child Drives You Crazy" author LeShan
18 Having need of a little more training: hyph.
21 Logical lead-in
22 Wife of "Modern Times" star
23 Hanging down loosely
26 Grammy-winner Braxton
27 ___ chi ch'uan
28 Concluding part of a racecourse: 2 wds.
33 Geologic time unit
34 Muscle problem
35 Money for the future, for short
36 Sit-up focus, briefly
37 Person who extracts metal from ore
39 Greek island
40 Bivouac
41 Bread buy
42 Capital of New South Wales, Australia

Down

1 Children's author Eleanor
2 Courage
3 Item used to sweep the floor
4 Former Kansas City Royals batting coach Charley
5 Standing against
6 Latest hours for vacating a hotel room: 2 wds.
7 "A Song Flung Up to Heaven" writer Maya
8 Boisterous girls, once
9 Historic Spanish fleet
13 Reagan-era proposal, initially
19 Concave navel, slangily
20 Military V.I.P., slangily
23 Large sandwich: 2 wds.
24 As one: 2 wds.
25 Theft
26 John Paul Young song, "Love is in ___": 2 wds.
29 Ave. crossers
30 Cronus or Oceanus
31 ___ de menthe
32 Mythological creature with a woman's head and bird's body
38 Calculator feature, initially

147

Across

1 ___ prima (painting technique)
5 Easter accessory
11 Fiddle middle?
12 Beethoven's Third
13 Feedbag fill
14 One leading a cheer, perhaps
15 Like early movies
17 Volunteer's statement: 2 wds.
19 Speaker of baseball
22 Hotelier Helmsley
23 Pre-entree course
25 Creative drive
26 Law in France
27 "Wake Up, Little ___"
30 Sink-unclogging brand
32 Cooped (up)
33 "Gremlins" actress Phoebe
34 Holy place
36 Fine fur
39 Place to get an espresso
42 Enter, as data: 2 wds.
43 "Love ___ the Air" (John Paul Young song): 2 wds.
44 Prime
45 Fender blemish

Down

1 Shakespearean fuss
2 Pastoral setting
3 Releases: 2 wds.
4 Pass out homework
5 "Let It ___" (Everly Brothers hit): 2 wds.
6 Praying figures
7 Cosa ___
8 Managua's country, for short
9 Earth-friendly prefix
10 Tit for ___
16 Mauna ___ (Hawaiian volcano)
17 France's ___ d'Hyères
18 Promotion: 2 wds.
20 Nervous: 3 wds.
21 Chalon-sur-___, city SSW of Dijon
24 God, in Guadalajara
28 Deep down
29 Like some cuisine
30 601, to Caesar
31 Inedible, like butter
35 Landlord's due
36 Hospital areas, initially
37 Riddle-me-___
38 Bad, in Barcelona
40 Shark's feature
41 Suffix with differ

148

Across

1 Lets go of
6 Closing act?
10 In the air
11 Bard
12 Flagship of Columbus: 2 wds.
14 Demolition ball alternative, initially
15 Best Musical of 1995–6
16 Away from the bow
17 "And don't forget…"
21 Darwin's interest
25 "But of course!"
26 Overhangs
27 Milk dispenser
29 "… ___ he drove out of sight"
30 Equipment of a horse for riding
32 Moist and cold
34 Electronics brand, for short
35 Chills and fever
37 Many a corp. hire
40 Arsonist
43 Thick reference book
44 Kind of power
45 Jewish month
46 Irregularly notched

Down

1 Play group
2 Flamboyance
3 Mom's warning
4 Little wriggler
5 Five-armed sea creature
6 Bridge measurement
7 Blood line
8 Hawaiian necklace
9 Pilot's announcement, for short
13 Distribute, with "out"
16 Air hero
18 Stow, as cargo
19 Bruce Springsteen's "___ the One"
20 Crew members
21 Caraway
22 Plane-jumping G.I.
23 All tied
24 Come to an end
28 ___ test ("Law & Order" evidence)
31 Cuckoo pint, e.g.
33 Fate
36 Migrant
37 Otis's movie partner
38 Meadow sounds
39 A lot of lot
40 Class-conscious grp.
41 Hebrew letter
42 "Neither a borrower ___ a lender be"

149

Across

1 GPS setting: 2 wds.
8 Dr. J's first pro league
11 ___ non grata
12 Console for playing Super Mario Bros., initially
13 Wimbledon footwear: 2 wds.
15 Architect Saarinen
16 Rock opera about a "pinball wizard"
17 Nostradamus, for one
18 More chichi
19 6-point plays, for short
20 Drink after a shot of alcohol
21 Spacious, as a car's interior
22 Woody Allen's partner
24 Korean soldier
27 Butting heads: 2 wds.
28 "Billy Budd" captain
29 2005 "Survivor" locale
30 Small woods
31 Cold War symbol: 2 wds.
33 Diamond stat.
34 Catherine the Great, e.g.
35 French marshal in the Napoleonic Wars (1769–1815)
36 Applied a patch: 2 wds.

Down

1 Best suited
2 Staggered
3 Golfer Els and comic Kovacs
4 "Up" actor Ed
5 Churn
6 Part of Q & A, briefly
7 Deli order
8 Social breakdown
9 Pricy wheels, slangily
10 From Nineveh: abbr.
14 ___-totsy
18 Sailor's greetings
20 Leads
21 Flying monster of film
22 Keep food from
23 Study of birds' eggs
24 Not outstanding
25 "Twelfth Night" lover
26 "Dr. Strangelove" actor Wynn
27 Beelike
28 "À ___ santé!"
30 Crop of birds
32 Finish, with "up"

150

Across

1. 1836 battle site
6. Beseech
11. Fiesta food
12. 1965 King arrest site
13. Process of changing words from one language into another
15. Pre-1975 power agcy.
16. One, in Ulm
17. Mme., in Mexico City
18. Fifth-century date
19. Approved
20. Flier to Copenhagen, initially
21. Icy coating
23. Identical
25. Lower in rank
27. Some old records
29. Sammy Davis's "___ Can": 2 wds.
33. Court people, for short
34. "Now I get it!"
36. Bread served with saag aloo
37. Suffix with guitar or clarinet
38. Brick-carrying trough
39. Go after legally
40. Admit defeat: 3 wds.
43. Heights: abbr.
44. Big fads
45. Madras dresses
46. Hearing, taste or touch

Down

1. Hook up
2. Texas city
3. Spiny tree
4. Calendar abbr.
5. Bone: prefix
6. Good manners: 3 wds.
7. Court decision
8. "Aeneid" queen
9. Lacking ethical values
10. Carvey and Rohrabacher
14. Without hesitation: 3 wds.
22. Did laps
24. 180° turn, slangily
26. Unhappy spectator's cry: 2 wds.
27. Garam ___ (Indian spice mixture)
28. Stable worker
30. Naval officer
31. Fries quickly in a little hot fat
32. Living: 2 wds.
33. Cubes
35. Corp. homebase
41. 56, to Caesar
42. Abu Dhabi is its cap.

151

Across

1 Be a cast member of: 2 wds.
6 Lines made of twisted fibers
11 "Bustin' ___" (1981 Richard Pryor film)
12 Circa
13 Glaringly vivid and graphic
14 She was turned to stone, in a Greek myth
15 Chooses, with "for"
16 State
17 Serenade, e.g.
18 Old TV knob, briefly
19 Nod, maybe
20 Sharpshooter
22 Animal shelters
23 V.I.P.
25 In the sack
27 Sacred beetle of ancient Egypt
30 Dissenting votes
31 Cha, in England
32 Ague cousin
33 Cling
35 "Glengarry ___ Ross"
36 San ___ (California city)
37 Sticky blobs
38 Brilliant success
39 Obviously surprised
40 Rummy groupings
41 Boarded: 2 wds.

Down

1 Concedes
2 Clipped slip
3 Like some cats
4 Deity with cow's horns
5 "20,000 Leagues" harpooner ___ Land
6 Corporal punishment inflictor
7 Brief bio, on parting
8 Type of ice cream soda: 3 wds.
9 Irish city
10 Mounts
16 Anticipate
18 ___ and haw
21 Green bean, for example
22 "CSI" sample
24 South American wood sorrel
25 Wreath for the head
26 Part of a dress above the waist
28 City in northern Syria
29 Burner inventor
31 Brings (out)
34 "Goodness gracious!"
35 Bantu language
37 Joke

152

Across

1 Couples, briefly
4 Turn-of-the-century year
7 Federal agcy., 1946–75
8 Bygone money
13 Lat. or Lith., once
14 Quiet, muted
15 Expected to place, as in a tournament
17 Start of Massachusetts' motto
18 Thought: prefix
19 The gift ___: 2 wds.
20 Maturity
23 Guess: abbr.
24 Experienced soldier
26 Desert land: abbr.
28 Cutting tool set in an H-shaped frame
31 Ned ___ ("Henry IV Part 2" character)
33 Highest active volcano in Europe
34 ___ Vista
35 Former Soviet president Gromyko
37 Cook in lots of oil
39 Chats online with, briefly
40 Hillshire Brands company: 2 wds.
41 Doctor's bag
42 Avena sativa grain
43 Federal warning system, initially

Down

1 To be found at various places throughout the text
2 Plant also known as mignonette
3 Author of film scripts
4 Store's goods, for short
5 "Dang it!"
6 Wine bar order
9 Alphabet series
10 Prolonged refusal to eat: 2 wds.
11 Flat-topped lands
12 "Must we not pay ___ to pleasure, too?": Wilmot: 2 wds.
16 Capital of Qatar
19 Exaltedly poetic
21 Eyes, poetically
22 Tulsa sch. named for a televangelist
25 Agreed to, slangily
26 Modern-day tablets
27 Roman sandal
29 Blood condition
30 Belt sites
32 Auto parts giant, initially
35 Atlas stat
36 No, in Russia
38 "Alice" waitress

153

Across

1 Cold dessert
7 Here, in Le Havre
10 Group of three
11 ___ a good thing: 2 wds.
12 Charm
13 Cleave
14 Islamic weight
15 By the item
17 Early smartphone
18 Deserves it: 2 wds.
19 Bondman
20 Black key: 2 wds.
21 She hid the spies at Jericho
23 Generous
26 Absorbed
30 Adjust
31 Brightly colored fish
32 Blubber
34 "Dumb & Dumber" actress
35 Bounce
36 Building material
38 "___ Coming" (1969 hit)
39 Laugh lightly: hyph.
40 Ham, to Noah
41 Flip-chart homes

Down

1 Begins
2 At least: 2 wds.
3 Carpenter's tool
4 1791 legislation: 3 wds.
5 ___ out a living
6 "Be seein' ya": hyph.
7 "___ Doctor" (Dr. Dre/Eminem song): 3 wds.
8 Agree
9 Completely committed: 2 wds.
11 Dubliners may talk with them: 2 wds.
16 Galileo's birthplace
20 Bill amt.
22 ___ Domini
23 Coral ___, Fla.
24 Repetitive sounding Philippine city
25 Stringed instrument
27 Army helicopter
28 Kind of post
29 Violent struggles
33 Bone (prefix)
37 ___ Party Nation

154

Across

1 Ditches
6 Append: 2 wds.
11 Not together
12 Dancer Astaire
13 Singer who played Hattie Pearl in "The Butler": 2 wds.
15 Billion extension
16 "Never Let ___" (Clark Gable film): 2 wds.
17 Ending for insist
19 Kelley and Kesey
21 Okinawa port
23 The robbing of ships at sea
27 Shakespeare's theater
29 Successful job seeker
30 "The Born Loser" cartoonist Chip
32 Martin ___, 1930s Army bomber: 2 wds.
33 Children's author Blyton
35 Ending for steward
36 Library ID
39 Burn superficially
41 Infantryman: 2 wds.
45 Book after Daniel
46 Piles on
47 Lucy's best friend
48 Lace ornament

Down

1 Farm mother
2 Kick ___ fuss: 2 wds.
3 Long-distance running race
4 Toyota hybrid models
5 Bleak and desolate
6 Part of X-X-X
7 From which Eve was created: 2 wds.
8 "King David" star, 1985
9 Couturier Cassini
10 "Miss Independent" singer
14 Dickens's Uriah
17 Professional people: abbr.
18 Lioness in "The Lion King"
20 U.S. medical research agcy.
22 Person who is expected, but not present
24 Denoting an important route
25 So-so grades
26 Desires
28 Forever and a day
31 Japanese appetizer
34 Ms. Street of mystery
36 "___ Hollers Let Him Go" (Chester B. Himes novel): 2 wds.
37 Lampblack
38 Nonsense
40 "I Wouldn't Treat ___" (Bobby Bland song): 2 wds.
42 Mineo of movies
43 Ethnic group of Vietnam
44 Letter run

155

Across

1 Shin bone
6 "Zorba the Greek" author ___ Kazantzakis
11 French town
12 One of the official languages of India
13 Light ___ (floaty): 2 wds.
14 Fingers
15 Queeg's command
17 ___-One, stage name of Lawrence Parker
18 Arctic animal
20 Insurance giant
22 Ex ___ (out of nothing)
24 Paris airport
27 Packs tightly
28 Do ___ situation: 2 wds.
29 Evergreens
30 Detach with a hammer's claw
31 Aussie "bear"
33 Sample
34 Sack
36 Big Indian
38 Began
40 City on the Mohawk
43 "The Chronicles of Narnia" author C. S.
44 "Masters Without Slaves" author
45 Vernacular
46 "Fiddler on the Roof" role

Down

1 New Deal prog.
2 "___ for Iceberg": 2 wds.
3 2001 movie set in Somalia: 3 wds.
4 Hip bones
5 Overhead photos
6 Group of nine
7 Bank offering, initially
8 Wife of Kanye West: 2 wds.
9 ___ and terminer
10 Guff
16 Classic opener
18 Suffix with consist
19 Old money
21 Norse mythological being
23 "___ Excited" (Pointer Sisters hit): 2 wds.
25 53, to Caesar
26 Canine cry
28 Impaneled: 3 wds.
30 Suffix with form
32 "You ___ right!": 2 wds.
34 Fun time
35 "... ___ saw Elba": 2 wds.
37 Dip ___ in (test): 2 wds.
39 E-mail ID, in short
41 Kind of computer monitor, for short
42 Letters before a crook's name

156

Across

1 When a baby is expected to be born: 2 wds.

8 Border-crossing necessities

11 Rubs hard, roughens

12 "You Are ___ Alone"

13 Planet seen just before sunrise: 2 wds.

15 Put

16 Nut used in soda

17 Luncheon ender

18 In a fair way

20 Hush-hush govt. group

21 Superior skill

22 1957 Literature Nobelist Albert

23 Breaks free

26 Farmer's area of study: abbr.

29 Beyond the limit: 2 wds.

30 French girlfriend

31 Actor Cronyn, Joe Finley in "Cocoon"

32 Spelunkers

34 Beyond calculation

36 Roman 401

37 Begin a voyage: 2 wds.

38 Hirer's request letters

39 Pittsburgh giant corp.: 2 wds.

Down

1 Make moist

2 Horseshoe-shaped fasteners: hyph.

3 Slips

4 Move to music

5 Straight as ___ (honest): 2 wds.

6 1983 movie starring Robert Duvall: 2 wds.

7 Monogram of Mason mysteries

8 Recite without inflection

9 Factotums: hyph.

10 Deviates from a course

14 Depicts with bias

19 "You" in France

21 "___ Loves Mambo" (Perry Como song)

22 Sidewalk eateries

23 High standards

24 Noises

25 "Enter!": 2 wds.

26 One-celled creatures

27 When doubled, a song by Blondie

28 Put back on the market

30 "Halt, cease!," to a sailor

33 Nos. on checks

35 Facebook rival, initially

157

Across

1 Intelligent
4 Enjoy the rink
9 Seize
11 Lavish bestowal
12 Damsel's rescuer
13 English landscape painter (1775–1851)
14 Pertinent
16 Square dancer, perhaps
17 Bothers
21 In addition
25 UN anti-child-labor agcy.
26 Cantilevered window
27 Once more
29 At some point in the past
30 Christmas Eve fuel: 2 wds.
32 Color quality
34 Garden pond swimmer
35 Loud and resonant, with a mournful tone
40 Talk of the town?
43 Arab bigwig
44 Emotionally unavailable type
45 Ancient alphabetic symbol
46 Computer expert, slangily
47 "Get the picture?"

Down

1 Turkish official
2 Make ready, informally
3 Baseball field covering
4 Closed
5 "M*A*S*H" setting
6 Barley bristle
7 Athletic supporter?
8 Act like a human
10 Dance energetically
11 Fence feature
15 "It hurts to say…"
18 Clock face
19 Mélange
20 CD track, often
21 Dinghy or dory
22 As a result
23 Suffix for man, ten or pen
24 Beauty shop
28 ___ counter, radiation measurer
31 Decree
33 Geological span
36 Blossom from a bulb
37 Birds on some ranches
38 Opening time, maybe
39 Elder, e.g.
40 Barbecue site
41 Great serve, in tennis
42 ___-tac-toe

158

Across

1 Secret society
6 Prince Valiant's princess
11 Addams Family member
12 Spy's activity, for short
13 Country's Brooks
14 Actor Jeremy of "Reversal of Fortune"
15 Winter or spring
17 Business letter abbr.
19 "___ or lose it": 2 wds.
22 Links rental
23 Eye part
25 In this location: Span.
26 Mil. training academy
27 B.A. or B.S.
28 Come to pass
30 Follower of the news
31 Looks after
32 "When I Was ___" ("H.M.S. Pinafore" song): 2 wds.
33 Aziz of "Parks and Recreation"
35 River joining the Rhone
38 Sign of the zodiac
41 French clerics
42 Worked with hay
43 Chills out
44 Eyelid sores

Down

1 Committee sess.
2 "I have an idea!"
3 Capital: hyph.
4 Focused
5 Muslim honorific
6 Short solos
7 "How to Handle a Woman" lyricist
8 "The Name of the Rose" writer
9 Huge amount
10 Reply: abbr.
16 Triumph
17 Hail ___ (cry "Taxi!"): 2 wds.
18 Be silent, in music
20 Forever
21 "It Must Be Magic" singer ___ Marie
24 "Yes, there is ___!" (believer's statement): 2 wds.
26 Idiosyncrasy
29 Caught, like fish: 3 wds.
30 Cowboy's rope
34 Priestly garb
35 Mediterranean isl.
36 Bart Simpson's grandpa
37 No longer used, as a word: abbr.
39 Riddle-me-___
40 Pop-ups, usually: abbr.

159

Across

1 Fast-moving card game
5 Adulterate
11 Meltdown site
12 Gets used (to)
13 Orderly grouping
15 Get up
16 Kind of water
17 Dangerous snake
18 Cousin of an ostrich
21 Good deal
22 Kind of blocker
24 C2H6
26 Mushroom caps
28 Far from abundant
31 Short publications?
35 Black gold
36 Kitten's noise
38 Hipster
39 Albanian coins
41 Beyond the fringe
43 Say "Enough is enough!": 3 wds.
46 Cream container
47 Caroler's number
48 Rules over
49 Aardvark's fare

Down

1 Beetle considered divine by Ancient Egyptians
2 Full of holes: var.
3 Break into suddenly
4 Afternoon socials
5 Like a lot
6 Chemical ending
7 Mooches
8 Anatomical ring
9 Forward: 2 wds.
10 Country spread
14 Born, in some gossip columns
19 More than a scuffle
20 All-purpose truck, for short
23 Calendar abbr.
25 Self starter?
27 Booster tail
28 Fuse two pieces of metal
29 Bore through
30 Sodium, e.g.
32 Director's call
33 January's birthstone
34 Reinforces (oneself), as for a shock
37 Hardship
40 Ill-gotten gains
42 Bone in the arm
44 Canterbury can
45 Brief time periods

160

Across

1 Quagmire
6 Accra's land
11 Sharp mountain ridge, to Jacques
12 Fanatical
13 "Count me in": 3 wds.
14 Europe-Asia divider
15 Excessive
17 Cooper cars
18 Sluggers' hits: abbr.
21 "Already?": 2 wds.
25 Ghost word
26 Home care provider, initially
27 "Evita" narrator
28 Highest point
30 Hawaiian honeycreeper
31 "Cagney & ___"
33 Advice to the angry
38 George of "Star Trek"
39 Imitative behavior
40 Acrylic fiber
41 Negation mark in logic
42 Casual language
43 Not purchases

Down

1 Actor Oka of "Heroes"
2 "East of Eden" brother
3 Try, try again
4 Attacks
5 Wendy Wasserstein's "The ___ Chronicles"
6 Fish that spawns at high tide
7 Ride, so to speak
8 As blind as ___: 2 wds.
9 "Blue" or "White" river
10 Magazine pages, often: abbr.
16 Check out
18 Alias, in commerce, initially
19 Conk
20 Bathroom, in Bristol
22 Peruvian plant with edible tubers
23 Omega, to an electrician
24 "The Matrix" hero
26 Like the famous tower in Pisa, Italy
29 Attach, in a way: 2 wds.
30 Mr. Magoo's trait
32 French states
33 "Cosmos" author Sagan
34 Tulsa locale, briefly
35 Relate, as a story
36 "Das Lied von der ___"
37 Humorist Bill and comedian Louis
38 Fros' mates

161

Across

1 Saucer in the sky, shortly
4 Schoolboy
7 When it's broken, that's good
8 "Die Meistersinger" heroine
9 Hoover, for one
12 Coffee order: abbr.
13 Dizziness
15 Euterpe's sister
17 Situations
18 Hokkaido people
19 Challenge for a barber
20 Brings under control: 2 wds.
24 Dorm room, sometimes
25 Devoted
27 Wood sorrel
29 Keep company
32 Baptism, for one
34 Bounce back
35 Boring device
37 Chamber groups
38 Environmental science
40 Infomercials, e.g.
41 Bled, as colors
42 Afternoon snooze
43 Casual attire
44 Reversible body part, as it were
45 Cousin of -trix

Down

1 Erect
2 "___ Queene" (Spenser work)
3 Group, establishment
4 On or to the left prefix
5 Broadway, e.g.
6 Jeanne ___, French heroine
9 Break a connection with
10 "The X-files" extra
11 Go (along)
14 Cap
16 Air
21 Egg holder
22 U.N. agcy. concerned with working conditions
23 ___-compete agreement
26 Computer owner
27 Command
28 About
30 Oxford scholarship namesake
31 Chucks
33 Addition
36 "The ___ Ranger"
37 Label A or B, e.g.
39 "We'll have a ___ old time"

162

Across

1 Dressed like Siouxsie Sioux

5 "It don't ___ thing if it ain't got that swing": 2 wds.

10 Old English letters

11 "… women do ___ require?" (Blake): 2 wds.

12 "Cool!"

13 Do-nothings

14 Abbr. on a bank statement

15 Apt. ad figure

16 Cattle call

17 Balaam's mount

18 Skillful, competent

19 ___ de France

20 Delaware Indian

22 Doormat fiber

23 Expected, in a way: 2 wds.

25 Prefix meaning "height"

27 Dearest principles

30 Certain camera, for short

31 "___ man walks into a bar…": 2 wds.

32 ___ for tat

33 "Bali ___"

34 Very, in Veracruz

35 Nigerian native

36 English, in Spanish

38 Lawnmower brand that means "bull"

39 "Uh-uh!"

40 Catch

41 Form of Spanish "to be"

42 "___ quam videri" (North Carolina's motto)

Down

1 Agreeable

2 Danish city

3 "Incorrect!": 3 wds.

4 Presidential inits.

5 Center

6 Blow-up: abbr.

7 Improvements

8 ___ oil (cologne ingredient)

9 Echo

13 Domineering

15 "___ Men" (2010 movie)

21 Cuckoo bird

22 Bee follower

24 Event in "Saving Private Ryan": hyph.

25 Gleaming

26 South American plains

28 Early October babies

29 Line feeder, of a sort

31 Black-and-white ducks

37 Mauna ___, Hawaii

38 "The Waste Land" monogram

163

Across

1 Alley animal
4 Atlas abbr.
7 Mediocre: 3 wds.
9 Gym set: abbr.
12 Progress
13 Sound of satisfaction
14 "Go, ___!"
15 Exploitative type
17 Deodorant place
19 D-Day target town: 2 wds.
20 Artistic frame
21 Cleaver nickname
22 Coral ridges: abbr.
23 Basketball net holder
25 1950s political monogram
26 Winston Churchill's "___ Country": 2 wds.
28 Peg Bundy portrayer ___ Sagal
30 Prefix with graph
31 Despite the fact that: 2 wds.
33 Having bony plates on the skin
35 Robt. E. Lee, e.g.
36 "Baseball Sluggers" commemorative stamp honoree
37 Founder of Lima
39 Codebreaking arm of govt.
40 Apples' mismatches
41 "The Racer's Edge," initially
42 Down units: abbr.

Down

1 ___ del Sol
2 Consequences: 2 wds.
3 Fish roe paste that's pink
4 "The ___ Squad" ABC TV series
5 Abuse: 3 wds.
6 Accident investigating org.
8 Easily-fooled folks
9 Useless effort: 2 wds.
10 1986 Chris de Burgh song that hit #3: 4 wds.
11 ___ Tuesday
16 ___ port (computer outlet), initially
18 Ending for beef or bump
22 Turns in to the cops: 2 wds.
24 Dallas cager, for short
27 Fam. member
29 Indie band ___ and Sara
32 Dental ___
34 Grand story
38 Blast

164

Across

1 Stagehands
6 "Metamorphosis" protagonist Gregor
11 Checking account type: 2 wds.
12 Indo-European
13 Heretofore: 2 wds.
14 Airplane seat access
15 1990s Indian P.M.
16 African capital
18 New England sch., home of the Minutemen: 2 wds.
20 Teacher's deg.
23 Book of the Apocrypha
25 La ___ (fossil site)
26 "Me too!": 2 wds.
27 Cake part
28 Hosp. staffers
29 Inner part of a nut
30 Amphibious landing craft, initially
31 Foreword, for short
32 Flops, withers
34 Martin ___ Buren (8th president)
37 Celebrated Italian violin maker Nicolo
39 Opposition
41 Large house
42 It was ___ of the tongue: 2 wds.
43 Group of eight
44 Shocked with a device

Down

1 Snarl or growl
2 Santa ___, Calif.
3 "___ My Peaches (You'd Better Stop Shaking My Tree)" (Irving Berlin song): 4 wds.
4 "___-wee's Big Adventure"
5 Predetermined cost: 2 wds.
6 Swedish cars
7 "Tosca" tune
8 Detective fiction: 2 wds.
9 ___ soda
10 Chemical suffix
17 ___ Wednesday
19 Hr. divs.
21 "Groove Is in the Heart" singers ___-Lite
22 Clay-sand mixture
23 Actress Clayburgh
24 Ballpark figures
25 1990s Attorney General William
27 "Join me for a meal": 2 wds.
29 Chivalrous guy: abbr.
31 "But you said…!" response: 2 wds.
33 "___ Gift" (W. C. Fields movie): 2 wds.
35 Foreign pen pal
36 "___ Blue"
37 ___ , amas, amat
38 "Big" fast-food item
40 Code-cracking org.

165

Across

1 Coin flip call: abbr.
4 "Wanted" poster letters
7 Cat's-eye, e.g.
10 Break, make, or stake follower
11 Dark meat, e.g.
12 Pier gp.
13 Ill-thought-out: hyph.
16 Even (with): 3 wds.
17 "Consarn it!"
18 Affix, as a button: 2 wds.
19 "Goodnight" girl of song
20 ___ Fein
22 Howard of "American Graffiti"
23 Amphibious landing craft, initially
26 Cockpit abbr.
27 AARP members, briefly
28 ___ Lingus
29 Bygone depilatory
31 Floors
33 Country singer LeAnn
37 NBA part
38 "Li'l Abner" cartoonist: 2 wds.
39 Uninvited guest, say
41 Matchsticks game
42 One of Snow White's buddies
43 King, in Portugal
44 Microbrewery offering, perhaps
45 Farm mother
46 Broadway time zone, shortly

Down

1 Foil-wrapped Hostess products
2 Eddy who made money in the 1950s and 1960s
3 Boater material
4 Tirana residents
5 "Black Narcissus" star Deborah
6 ___ Khan
7 Teriyaki spices
8 ___ of Aquitaine
9 Tees off
14 Saga in verse
15 Ending for cloth or bombard
19 Weave
21 Atlanta Braves div.
23 Layered dish
24 Start out on a voyage: 2 wds.
25 "Would I steer you wrong?": 2 wds.
30 Forced movements
32 GPS heading, shortly
34 Champion skier Phil
35 Fencing equipment
36 Nautical pole
38 "...and pretty maids all in ___": 2 wds.
40 Do, re, mi letters

166

Across

1 Bonehead
6 Hourly pay
10 GMC pickup truck
12 IRS identifiers
13 Evil
14 Hit hard, slangily
15 Certain court hearings
17 Like some humor
18 Bread served with saag aloo
20 French annuity
22 Capitol Hill worker
24 Dog breed
27 Prettify oneself
29 Palindromic belief
30 Rubbernecking
32 He loved Lucy
33 Stravinsky and Sikorsky
35 "Wait a ___!": abbr.
36 Environmental prefix
38 Bleated
40 Prefix with phobic and lith
42 Sets of eight
45 Bidding site
46 Tattered along the edges
47 Thin (out)
48 Beasts of burden

Down

1 Away from NNE
2 Parisian pronoun
3 Not subject to limitations
4 Wasting time
5 High guy in Dubai: var.
6 One way to go: abbr.
7 Starts of Lents: 2 wds.
8 Watchdog's sound
9 Glimpse
11 Spot seller, for short: 2 wds.
16 Rotten little kid
18 Neighbor of 10-Across
19 Affectation
21 Follower of three- or pigeon-
23 Online issue
25 "___-majesté"
26 Suffix after "path" or "synth"
28 Difficulty: abbr.
31 ___ Empire (builders simulation game): 2 wds.
34 Pelvic bones
36 Big boss, for short
37 Island of the south central Philippines
39 Characters in "The Odyssey"
41 "Popeye" surname
43 Actor Billy ___ Williams
44 1960s campus grp.

167

Across

1 Natives of Nigeria
5 Breakfast order
11 Drone, e.g.
12 Son of William the Conqueror
13 "Girl With ___ Hat" (Vermeer): 2 wds.
14 Agreement
15 Place to buy rolls of tobacco: 2 wds.
17 Living dragon
18 24-hour endurance race locale: 2 wds.
21 Alaska's first governor
24 ___ belle étoile (in the open air): 2 wds.
25 "The Subject Was Roses" director Grosbard
26 Attention-getters
28 Heads
31 Family men
33 Fossilized marine animals
37 Haberdashery item: 2 wds.
38 "And here it is!": hyph.
39 Out of one's mind
40 Certain hosp. scans
41 Summarized or abridged
42 Doctors who check out head colds, for short

Down

1 Apple product
2 "Boss Lady" star Lynn
3 Cassini of fashion
4 Singer Neil
5 Divides
6 Odd-numbered page
7 Create a cryptogram
8 Discontinue a legislative session
9 Brontë's "Jane ___"
10 Old school comedian ___ Caesar
16 "A Beautiful Mind" director ___ Howard
18 ___ of luxury
19 1997 U.S. Open winner
20 Most old
22 1936 candidate Landon
23 Some fraternity men, initially
27 Cut with small quick strokes: 2 wds.
28 Copied gene for gene
29 New Test. book
30 Self-conscious question: 3 wds.
32 "Crazy" singer Patsy
33 Baseballer Martinez
34 Glacier-formed lake
35 Do magazine work
36 Be cheeky with
37 Service award

SOLUTIONS

1

```
A B B A S ■ ■ S A C
C A R L O S ■ E M U
C R O P P E R ■ A P R
R E T ■ R N A ■ B U S
A S H ■ A T H L E T E
■ ■ A N I ■ O D E S
■ D E C O M P O S E ■
L E A N ■ E L K ■ ■
A N T E N N A ■ E S P
U S A ■ I T S ■ R H O
D E B ■ L A T E R A L
E L L ■ ■ L I V E R Y
D Y E ■ ■ C A D I S
```

2

```
S A M S A ■ A B A T E
S T A N D ■ S A L O N
R E N E E ■ W H E R E
■ T A S T E ■ A S S
P A I D ■ A L A ■ ■
D B L ■ F O L K S Y
S A L L E ■ A C T E D
■ S A R A H S ■ R A E
■ ■ G R A ■ M A R E
L A C ■ L E R O I ■
A D A G E ■ F O N D A
D U M A S ■ D R E A R
D E E D S ■ S E R E S
```

3

```
A M O ■ S A S ■ D E A
G A P ■ C O T ■ R A M
S E A L A N E ■ A S P
■ E L E V ■ N E L
A I M E E ■ E A G L E
M G M T ■ A N C ■ ■
I N D I G E S T I O N
■ D A R ■ R I C E ■
Y A T E S ■ H E I S T
E T O ■ L B O S ■ ■
N E E ■ A I R S H I P
T A I ■ M A A ■ A R A
L M N ■ P S S ■ S E D
```

4

```
U S U R P S ■ S D S
M I S E R Y ■ S H O E
A G A M A S ■ T A M P
■ O U T R A G E ■
■ G I N S E N G ■
O H M S ■ M A E N A D
R I A T A ■ S W E A T
S A C R U M ■ H E R S
■ A T A T I M E ■
■ S E N O R A S ■
T A L C ■ A L P A C A
A L I E ■ C U E S T A
B A S ■ A S R A R E
```

5

```
A P O K E ■ A N A I S
L O R A X ■ B I R C H
A L E P H ■ E L S I E
N E G L I G E E ■ ■
■ ■ A B O ■ S A M S
A S I N I N E ■ D E E
C E N ■ T D S ■ A N E
H A M ■ B O T C H U P
E L E V ■ L I A ■ ■
■ A D A M S A L E ■
S H A L E ■ A U R A L
B O G E Y ■ T A M I L
A S S T S ■ E L E N A
```

6

```
A L O F T ■ ■ V A T
L A G O O N ■ T O R A
I M A R E T ■ A T M S
G O U T ■ H A B E A S
H U G H ■ T A R D E
T R E E ■ M I S S A L
■ ■ R E B E C ■ ■
B O D E G A ■ O A K S
A R A C E ■ S N E E
I G N O R E ■ A D E E
L A I R ■ S L U R P S
O N E D ■ D E C E I T
R A L ■ ■ Y E S N O
```

7

```
A T S E A ■ P A T I O
S W A R M ■ A D O R E
P A R R Y ■ L I N E R
■ C O L L I E ■ ■
S T A R ■ U S U R E R
C O S ■ D N A ■ E R E
A P T ■ R E D ■ V A N
L E I ■ A T E ■ U S E
D E C E I T ■ F L E W
■ ■ K N E L L S ■
S E P I A ■ O U I J A
A M O N G ■ S T O U P
N U D G E ■ S E N S E
```

8

```
T E A ■ A U F ■ A D O
I M P ■ G N U ■ R I G
C U R T A I N C A L L
■ I O T A ■ A B L E
P H O N E T I C S ■
O U R ■ ■ E R A ■ ■
D E I C E ■ K O R A N
■ L A H ■ ■ A C E
■ M E T E O R I T E
T H A W ■ A X E L ■
S E N S I T I V I T Y
A R E ■ R E D ■ N A E
R E S ■ E R E ■ G I N
```

SOLUTIONS

9

```
E T C H █ █ D O U B T
Y A H O O █ U L N A R
E N E M Y █ G I P S Y
█ █ D E E R █ O R S O
S A D █ R O T █ E O N
E G A D █ L E A D █ █
C O R R E L A T I O N
█ █ C Y S T █ E C H O
R A H █ T O N █ T O W
O P E D █ P A R A █ █
A R E A L █ B A B E L
D I S C O █ S I L L Y
S L E E T █ D E L E █
```

10

```
W A X █ M G S █ N E B
A B M █ T I E █ A I R
I R A █ E R A S U R E
F I R S T L E T T E R
█ K I N █ E R I █ █
T E S T A █ L I C I T
R A T T █ P A S A █ █
U N H I P █ A I L E Y
█ E G S █ R E M █ █
W A S H E R D R I E R
N E P T U N E █ L G E
B O O █ D A N █ E I N
A N T █ O S T █ S S A
```

11

```
M Y O P I C █ █ S U P
P O T A T O █ P P S S
H U B C A P █ I E S T
█ █ I N T E G E R S █
A S O F █ S L O █ █
L O R I S █ L U C A S
T I N C T █ I T C H Y
A R E C A █ S O L O N
█ █ O R A █ N I T S
B E P A R T O F █ █
U T E S █ E L O I S E
L A I T █ A D O R E E
G S N █ R E D E A L
```

12

```
D A F T █ A L L O W S
U G L I █ G A U C H O
C H A M B E R L A I N
T A M I L █ G U S T S
█ █ D I K E █ █
A N G I N A █ E D D A
D I S T I N C T I O N
S L A Y █ J O H N N Y
█ █ D I M E █ █
S A L V O █ E R O D E
E Q U I L A T E R A L
T U R B O S █ A S K S
T A K E R S █ L O S E
```

13

```
B A R S █ R U S S O
A L O E █ T I N I E R
N E A R █ H O W L E R
G E N E R A T I O N █
█ █ N I N E S █ █
B A S E D █ R E H A B
U S A █ █ E R E
S P E C S █ T H R E E
█ █ H U S S Y █ █
█ S P A R E P A R T S
T H R I F T █ D I A L
N O O S E S █ E C R U
T O P E R █ S E E M
```

14

```
A P E R C U █ O D D S
D O R I A N █ W E R E
S L E E P W A L K E R
█ L E A F █ A W E
C L A S S R O O M █
A I R █ R O W E R S
P E R I P A T E T I C
O N E M A N █ E M U
█ S P U T T E R E D
P I T █ S A U L █
O L I V E B R A N C H
M I N I █ L I N E A R
P A G E █ E N D O W S
```

15

```
█ A L G I D █ O V A
█ P E A C E █ M I L
█ T Y R A N N I Z E
█ █ B O S U N █ █
P A S S █ L O B E S
O F T █ B L U R R Y
P R O G R E S S I O N
P O O L E D █ E D O
A S P I C █ B R E D
█ █ S U R G E █ █
█ P A T R I A R C H
█ O W E █ S I N A I
█ E E N █ K N E L T
```

16

```
L A V A █ C O A S T S
Y V E S █ O H D E A R
S E R T █ N A V A J O
█ █ S E V E R E █ █
Y E A R S █ A N S A
E A T N O █ S T U N G
O V I █ █ G A I
W E L S H █ A P A I N
█ D E M O █ M A R L A
█ █ I R E F U L █ █
M T E T N A █ L O R I
A R C H E S █ V A I N
P I G S T Y █ I F N I
```

SOLUTIONS

17

```
R I D G E . L A C T I
O N E A D . E I L A T
W I N T E R G R E E N
. . O L E . B O L O .
C A B S . M D A . . .
A L A . O B E S E L Y
S I L V E R B E L L S
A I M E D A T . I B E
. . S S N . U S S R .
S C O T . D E R . . .
C H R I S T M A S S Y
A G O G O . I L O N A
N E N E H . T S L O T
```

18

```
A R R A S . H O S E
G E E U P . L A R K S
A L I K E . A W A I T
M I N . C A W . T E A
A N I . S P Y . O R T
S E N T . H E A R S E
. . A P A R T . . .
T H E I R S . M A L E
W E N . I I I . S I M
O L D . S A D . H A M
B E A D S . E E R I E
I N L A Y . A V A S T
T A L K . L A M E S
```

19

```
S C A L P . S T E E D
A L L O Y . E R I E S
R O T O R . M A N E S
. T A K E S I D E S .
. . A S O N E . .
M O S T . T A R T A R
A U K . S H R . S A B
S T A T U E . B O S S
. . E R R O R . .
. S H A P E L E S S .
E L I S A . D A T E D
L I F E S . A T R E E
A M I S S . S H O A T
```

20

```
S A N T . C A S S I A
A L O E . O U T E A T
L I N A . E N I G M A
E S P . E N T R . . .
S T A S I . I F O L D
. R N S . E R R O R .
A S E A . I O N S .
A L I K E . C E Y .
R O L E O . C S P A N
. . B C A R . L I I
S O V I E T . C A M E
A C C T N O . E T A L
S T R E E P . L A T S
```

21

```
S O M A S . C G I
I C I C L E . S H U T
T A L C U M . T I R E
. . O R I G A N U M
. L A M P R E Y .
P A L P . S L I P O N
O V O L O . S N O R E
P A T I N A . G O G O
. . S C R A P P Y
H I T H E R T O
O B O E . O R W E L L
P I E D . W I E N I E
I D S . . A R E T E
```

22

```
S I B S . L E G A T O
C N E T . I N E S S E
O F N O . E S T H E R
R U E . O N U S . .
E N D O W . E R A S E
. I R E . D I M E S
R E C D . D I S C
A N T I S . B O N .
F L I N T . O F O L D
. A R T S . A A R
R O D N E Y . A C R O
S P A C E K . N I C O
S T P E T E . A D H D
```

23

```
J A W . R A N . .
U S A . O D E . F I N
I L L . C Z A R I N A
C O D A S . P O R T O
E P O S . . D E E M
S E R I A L S . S R I
. F A R E A S T .
H A S . C U T L A S S
O R A L . . A T O P
M O L A R . S P I N E
E M A N A T E . O N E
D A D . D O N . N E D
. . S O T . S T Y
```

24

```
L A P . M O B I L E
E L I E . I N R O A D
T O N I . D O I N G S
S T O L I D . . .
. . T A M L A . S E L
G E N T E E L . W G A
E X O . L E U . E I S
R P I . D A M P E S T
M O R . A S N O T .
. . . T I N P A N
O N T A P E . T E T E
H E A T E R . S A I D
M A R L I N . S E S
```

SOLUTIONS

25

S	E	N	N	A		I	F	T	H	E
C	R	O	O	N		D	E	W	A	R
H	O	R	S	E		E	D	I	T	S
	M	I	S	S		E	C	H	T	
P	A	A	R		C	E	R	E		
I	G	N		R	O	T	A	T	E	S
C	U	C	K	O	O	C	L	O	C	K
T	A	O	I	S	T	S		L	O	Y
	U	L	E	E		I	D	L	E	
A	H	S	O		R	E	S	T		
R	A	I	T	A		A	N	A	I	S
A	M	N	O	T		S	E	L	L	S
Y	E	S	N	O		T	R	E	E	T

26

M	A	C	E	D		T	B	S	P	S
A	N	O	T	E		S	A	N	A	A
M	A	R	C	C	H	A	G	A	L	L
M	G	D		O	A	R		P	A	L
A	R	O		R	E	I	S	S	U	E
L	A	B	S		C	N	N			
	M	A	S	C		A	U	R	A	
	G	A	I		B	O	C	A		
H	O	S	T	E	S	S		S	A	B
A	B	O		S	L	Y		E	D	O
S	E	L	F	A	S	S	U	R	E	D
A	S	F	A	R		O	W	E	M	E
T	E	A	M	S		P	E	D	E	S

27

T	U	B		B	A	A		B	I	G
A	G	E		A	L	F	A	L	F	A
P	L	A	S	T	E	R	C	A	S	T
S	I	D	E		O	R	C			
		W	A	G		E	K	E	S	
	F	L	E	X	E	S		T	A	I
C	L	A	R	I	N	E	T	I	S	T
R	A	P		S	U	R	R	E	Y	
T	W	I	T		S	E	A			
	D	A	T		C	A	M	E		
W	E	A	R	A	N	D	T	E	A	R
E	N	R	O	U	T	E		R	N	A
B	E	Y		T	H	Y		Y	E	S

28

A	G	A	M	E		P	I	E	T	A
S	N	A	I	L		A	R	N	E	L
S	A	N	A	A		R	A	I	T	A
O	R	D		I	V	E		G	A	M
C	L	E	A	N	E	R		M	N	O
	D	E	T		E	A	U	S		
	C	E	A	S	E	L	E	S	S	
B	O	T	H		R	A	O			
A	C	E		C	A	R	C	A	S	S
S	H	S		A	N	G		L	P	N
A	L	I	A	S		E	L	L	I	E
L	E	A	S	T		S	I	E	T	E
T	A	N	I	S		S	A	Y	E	R

29

B	A	I	T		S	A	L	A	D	A
A	N	T	I		E	N	A	M	O	R
S	T	E	P		A	D	R	A	T	E
T	A	S	T	E	T	E	S	T	S	
			O	B	E	S	E			
S	H	R	E	W	D		N	A	D	A
P	A	T						M	A	G
R	T	E	S		S	A	H	I	B	S
			P	I	N	Z	A			
	H	O	R	S	E	T	R	A	D	E
D	E	F	I	L	E		A	R	A	L
E	L	A	T	E	R		S	I	D	S
N	I	N	E	T	Y		S	A	S	E

30

S	E	M	I	S		S	O	L	E	D
A	L	I	S	T		T	R	O	P	E
G	A	M	M	A		E	A	T	I	N
A	N	E	S	T	H	E	T	I	C	
			E	U	R	O				
I	C	I	C	L	E		R	O	O	D
T	O	D	A	Y		C	I	R	C	A
D	O	S	S		B	A	O	B	A	B
			S	M	U	T				
	P	L	E	A	S	A	N	T	L	Y
S	O	O	T	Y		L	O	U	I	E
P	O	R	T	O		P	E	N	N	A
A	L	D	E	R		A	L	G	E	R

31

B	B	C		S	I	M	P	L	E
R	O	L	E		P	R	O	V	E	N
A	R	I	L		R	E	A	C	T	S
W	A	P	I	T	I					
	J	O	H	N	S		B	O	D	
F	O	O	T	A	G	E		A	A	H
O	B	I		N	B	C		C	H	A
E	O	N		K	A	R	A	K	U	L
S	E	T		S	L	E	E	P		
		A	T	R	E	S	T			
S	L	O	G	A	N		I	D	E	A
H	E	R	O	I	C		E	A	R	L
H	U	R	T	L	E		L	E	K	

32

S	A	D	A		S	C	R	A	P	E
I	C	E	S		C	R	A	T	E	R
G	R	A	S	S	H	O	P	P	E	R
N	O	D	U	H		C	A	S	K	S
			R	I	A	S				
A	N	D	E	R	S		T	M	E	N
S	I	E	R	R	A	L	E	O	N	E
A	P	P	S		N	O	S	A	L	E
			P	A	C	T				
E	D	A	T	E		U	A	N	D	I
V	A	C	A	N	T	S	T	A	R	E
I	N	I	T	I	O		O	S	I	S
L	O	S	I	N	G		R	A	P	T

SOLUTIONS

33

```
C E S T . . P U P A E
A N E R A . A T R I A
R U L E S . R E A R S
A R F . S O O . C C I
F E A R N O T . T O N
E S S A . H I D I N G
. S K A L D I C .
S H E E N A . D A I S
A E R . A L F A L F A
F A T . P A R . J O Y
A R I S E . I R O N Y
R O O T S . A N K L E
I F N O T . D E Y S
```

34

```
D A B . C A T
O U R . O V A . P E G
G R E E T E R . L A O
M O A N S . T I A R A
A R K S . D I E T
S A T . C A L E N D S
. H A P L E S S .
P A R F A I T . A S P
A N O A . M I T E
U T U R N . G A L A S
L E G . A C O N I T E
A S H . P A N . N U T
. E Y E . G S A
```

35

```
A N I . R Y A . S L Y
C E N T A U R . T A O
R E F O R M A T O R Y
E M O T E . B U N K O
. A B Y S S E S .
T H A L I A . H A P S
W E N . T H E . G U T
O L D S . O R N E R Y
. S A P P O R O .
D I N A R . A P I A N
I N T R A C T A B L E
E K E . D A I L I E S
T I S . O R C . S E T
```

36

```
A A N D E . A D E A D
S L E E P . R O L L E
T E N N I S E L B O W
I F A T . T W E E T Y
. I N R E D .
A R I S T A . A R G
S O U T H W E S T E R
A B M . B E E T L E
. P R O N G .
A N N A L S . O G R E
Y O U R E S O V A I N
E R N E S . T I M O N
S A N D S . T A S T E
```

37

```
J A R S . C O O P
A L E E . F A U N A
M O A N . M A R T E N
B E R I B E R I .
. R O E S . E L A N
H A R E S . S A G O
E O N . B I O . B A T
E R G S . E R R O R
K N E E . U S E R
. T H R O W I N S
S T A T U S . R O I L
H A R E M . A U T O
Y O K E . P S S T
```

38

```
P A C A . B D R M
A G E S . N A I A D
I N S T . M O R A S S
L I T E R A T I .
. L R O N . U N I S
F R A N C E . M O R E
L I V . K A T . S O N
A S I T . T H E E N D
B E E R . E A R P
. A I R D R I E S
S E T U P S . A E R O
E D E M A . N C I S
E M M A . D E C A
```

39

```
A B I D E . K S T A R
R A N I N . U T E R O
A D D E D . D O L C E
L E E S . J O W L
. F I L A S . T R A
P H A S E I . A A S
E A T . D A B . L E S
A R I . L A T E S T
R P G . M A R S H
. A C A I . T E L E
L A B O R . B R A I N
A L L O T . E A R L Y
B E E N A . A P T T O
```

40

```
P E T I T . T O R U S
E V A D E . A R E T E
L I C I T . L I N A C
F L O O R C L O T H
. C A R O L .
P L O Y . T W E L V E
E E R . A I M
A U B U R N . O C A S
. P O I L U .
R U M B L E S E A T
M A N O R . A T R I A
A V I S O . S E G N O
G E T T Y . T R O T S
```

SOLUTIONS

41

```
O T R O S   S E T A N
P O I L U   C A I N E
T R A N S P A R E N T
S E L   H O T   R E T
T A T   I S M   E A L
O T O S   S A D D L E
      S C E N A
P A P E R S   S T A R
A S E   O S O   O D E
S T R   W E D   U H S
T H I R D D E G R E E
E M O T E   S T E R N
L A D E D   A S R E D
```

42

```
A S T E W   I R E N A
C L O T H   N O N O S
D O G C A T C H E R S
C P A   T A O   R I N
      O N E G I G
P E T R O L   N I P S
A S E A T   N A Z I S
H A M M   M I N E T A
      P A L A C E
A Y E   I R T   P A Y
B A R R E L A L O N G
E L E N I   T O N T O
D U R A N   E L D E R
```

43

```
A E S O P   T A I G A
S L U M S   O M N E S
C A P E T   P A C T S
O P E N   B E H O M E
T S R   T A R   N A S
S E A M U S   B V D S
    B E A T S M E
S M U T   I C I N G S
T A N   P O I   I O C
A D D S O N   N E V A
B R A N S   B O N E R
L A N E S   S A C R E
E S T E E   A M E N D
```

44

```
H O U N D   L I S
A C T I I I   O N E
H E L L E N E   U F C
A A E   C T A   D R U
S N Y   A E R A T O R
    I S L   S I N E
  B I G T I C K E T
F A N E   N O S
E G O T I S M   T E C
R J R   L I P   A V A
R O D   O D O A C E R
I B E   E S C O R T
S S R   T A S S E
```

45

```
S O L O S   A N I L S
Q U A R T   S E R A L
U T T E R   P O R N O
A L I   I C E   E D O
B E N   V I N   C A P
S T A V E S   P L U S
  M E N   P E A
I B E X   M A R I N E
N O R   M A S   M O N
S U I   O P T   A D D
I N C U R   I M B U E
S C A L P   M U L L A
T E N T H   E M E E R
```

46

```
W I T   N A B   A M U
A D U   S E I S M A L
L E T O F F S T E A M
L O U P   T A R
    T O M   S I B S
  D E E D E E   C E E
W E D D I N G B A N D
C M I   E L A I N E
S O F A   O L D
    I S U   U P A T
T I C K L E D P I N K
E L E A N O R   T A O
M A S   A S U   Y D S
```

47

```
C R T   S K I   A L P
O U R   T I S   N E O
L E I   A D R E N A L
A D A P T   A L O N E
    L E U   E M U
C H A P S   L Y N C H
I O N   C O O
A D D L E   S I E G E
    E O N   A I M
T H R U M   T I E R S
A I R T I M E   N A E
P R O   T O E   T N T
E E R   Y O N
```

48

```
A M A   I P O   A B U
G O S   D I C T I I O N
T R O J A N H O R S E
S O F A   O P P
    D N A   S L A B
  S P E E D S   A M C
B I R D B R A I N E D
I C I   R I N G E R
B A C O   P O L
    E C G   O B I T
M O T H E R G O O S E
E D A S N E R   B E E
D E G   A A E   O E N
```

SOLUTIONS

49

C	U	F	F	S			A	C	M	E
U	N	R	I	P	E		S	L	I	M
E	D	I	T	O	R		H	A	L	O
S	O	D		O	R	B		S	I	T
T	E	G		L	O	O	K	S	E	E
A	R	E	A		R	H	E	S	U	S
		F	C	C		R	E	T		
B	E	R	T	H	S		P	R	A	T
O	N	E	S	E	L	F		U	G	H
A	T	E		N	A	E		G	E	E
S	I	Z	E		M	A	G	G	O	T
T	R	E	K		S	T	E	L	L	A
S	E	R	E			S	L	E	D	S

50

I	R	E		E	R	R			
S	E	X		D	O	E		D	E	B
O	T	T		G	E	N	T	I	L	E
P	A	R	T	Y		O	S	S	I	A
O	K	A	Y			P	I	T	S
D	E	S	P	O	I	L		N	E	T
	P	E	R	S	I	S	T	
A	L	E		E	M	B	L	E	M	S
B	A	C	H			O	G	E	E
B	R	I	A	R		F	E	R	A	L
E	V	A	S	I	V	E		A	L	L
S	A	L		F	I	N		T	I	E
		T	A	D		E	E	R

51

P	C	B		C	C	S		
A	H	A		O	U	T	C	A	S	T
N	E	L		R	E	P	L	E	T	E
T	R	A	P	P		A	S	A	S
E	I	N	S		D	E	P	O	R	T
D	E	C	I	B	E	L		P	E	S
	E	S	P	N	E	W	S	
H	E	S		O	N	E	O	F	U	S
A	S	H	L	E	Y		K	A	N	E
U	S	E	E		W	E	B	E	R
T	E	E	N	A	G	E		L	A	G
E	N	T	I	T	L	E		E	S	E
	C	O	P		S	E	I

52

M	I	R	E		E	L	O	P	E	D
O	N	E	D		M	A	D	A	M	A
E	N	T	E	R	T	A	I	N	E	R
S	E	A	L	Y		C	O	R	N
H	E	R		E	A	U		U	G	A
A	D	D	L		S	L	A	T	E	Y
		D	A	T	U	M		
S	T	O	L	L	E		U	P	U	P
A	R	M		A	P	I		O	N	O
H	A	E	C		P	A	L	E	S
I	L	L	U	S	I	O	N	I	S	T
B	E	E	R	Y	S		A	S	C	I
S	E	T	T	L	E		S	H	O	T

53

K	E	P	I		A	R	I	S	E	S
I	L	L	D	O	M	Y	B	E	S	T
P	O	A	C	H	E	D	E	G	G	S
	T	A	R	R	E	R	
	H	O	R	O		R	I	N	K	Y
R	A	N	D	B		S	A	O	N	E
D	W	I			R	U	N
A	S	S	A	M		P	I	T	T	S
S	E	T	T	O		A	S	H	E
	M	O	B	C	A	P	
R	E	S	O	L	U	T	I	O	N	S
C	A	E	S	A	R	S	A	L	A	D
A	P	A	T	H	Y		H	E	M	I

54

A	S	S	A	M		R	A	K	E	R
M	A	T	R	I		A	M	A	R	E
B	R	A	G	A		T	I	N	E	S
L	E	T	O		C	E	S	S	N	A
E	E	E		B	A	R		A	O	L
	S	O	F	A	S		A	S	W	E
	F	A	S	T	C	A	R	
A	T	T	A		L	I	R	A	S
L	A	H		D	E	A		I	O	S
A	R	E	N	A	S		A	D	I	A
S	T	A	C	Y		A	L	E	R	S
K	A	R	A	N		C	E	R	E	S
A	N	T	R	E		C	A	S	E	Y

55

C	C	L	E	F		S	W	A	G	E
O	R	A	R	E		H	A	L	E	D
M	I	L	L	I	S	E	C	O	N	D
E	S	A		N	A	P		M	I	I
A	T	L		T	V	S		A	A	E
T	O	A	T	E	E		U	R	L	S
		E	D	S	E	L		
T	E	C	S		T	S	T	R	A	P
U	T	E		C	I	S		A	P	R
R	E	M		A	M	E		M	O	A
G	R	E	E	N	E	N	E	R	G	Y
I	N	N	E	S		C	O	O	E	E
D	E	T	O	O		E	N	D	E	R

56

P	R	O	M	O		P	I	P	E	T
U	N	G	A	R		E	M	E	E	R
M	A	R	I	A	H	C	A	R	E	Y
A	S	E		L	E	T	T	
		G	E	R	I		C	H	G
	H	A	R	D	N	O	S	E	D
A	L	A	I			R	C	M	P
S	P	A	N	G	L	I	S	H	
A	N	S		I	T	N	O	
		L	A	R	A		P	J	S
U	N	C	O	N	S	C	I	O	U	S
A	T	E	I	T		A	R	R	A	N
W	H	E	N	S		B	A	N	N	S

SOLUTIONS

57

B	U	S	E	S	■	A	R	Y	A	N
O	R	A	T	E	■	M	O	O	S	E
L	I	G	H	T	W	E	I	G	H	T
A	C	A	I	■	I	N	L	A	Y	S
■	■	C	U	D	D	Y	■	■	■	■
A	B	L	A	Z	E	■	■	L	A	O
A	E	O	L	I	A	N	H	A	R	P
H	E	W	■	■	N	I	E	C	E	S
■	■	D	O	G	M	A	■	■	■	■
M	A	N	U	A	L	■	T	R	I	M
A	P	O	S	T	E	R	I	O	R	I
T	E	N	T	H	■	U	N	P	I	N
T	R	E	S	S	■	E	G	E	S	T

58

E	N	U	R	E	■	A	F	T	E	R
B	E	R	E	A	■	S	O	A	V	E
B	E	E	P	S	■	K	O	R	E	A
S	M	A	R	T	S	■	D	O	R	M
■	■	■	E	S	T	O	P	■	■	■
B	A	S	H	■	Y	A	R	R	O	W
O	R	I	E	L	■	T	O	I	L	E
T	E	N	N	E	R	■	C	O	D	E
■	■	■	S	E	N	S	E	■	■	■
H	I	F	I	■	A	N	S	W	E	R
A	D	O	B	E	■	O	S	A	K	A
F	E	L	L	A	■	R	O	G	E	T
T	A	K	E	R	■	T	R	E	S	S

59

E	M	S	■	S	K	A	■	S	P	Y
N	A	N	■	W	A	R	■	I	L	E
T	R	A	D	I	T	I	O	N	A	L
E	G	R	E	S	S	■	A	C	C	T
R	O	L	E	S	■	F	R	E	E	S
■	■	■	M	A	C	E	■	R	B	I
D	P	S	■	L	E	E	■	E	O	N
I	R	E	■	P	E	L	F	■	■	■
S	I	L	A	S	■	S	E	T	I	N
M	O	L	Y	■	B	O	L	E	R	O
I	R	O	N	C	U	R	T	A	I	N
S	T	U	■	C	T	R	■	S	N	O
S	O	T	■	L	A	Y	■	E	A	S

60

A	L	O	N	G	■	N	I	N	T	H
R	I	F	L	E	■	E	M	O	R	Y
R	E	F	E	R	■	E	A	T	U	P
A	N	Y	■	A	N	D	■	H	S	N
U	S	O	■	L	U	S	■	I	T	O
■	■	U	S	D	T	■	O	N	E	I
C	U	R	I	O	■	P	A	G	E	D
I	N	R	E	■	D	I	R	T	■	■
T	S	O	■	S	E	C	■	O	L	E
A	T	C	■	O	A	K	■	L	O	L
D	A	K	A	R	■	S	T	O	G	Y
E	G	E	S	T	■	O	A	S	I	S
L	Y	R	E	S	■	N	I	E	C	E

61

N	O	S	E	■	W	A	R	G	O	D
U	G	L	Y	■	A	L	U	M	N	A
T	R	U	E	■	L	E	N	T	E	N
S	E	R	F	■	K	E	N	■	■	■
■	■	■	U	R	I	■	Y	A	M	S
A	P	P	L	I	E	D	■	L	E	U
G	U	E	S	S	T	I	M	A	T	E
E	R	A	■	C	A	B	A	R	E	T
S	E	L	F	■	L	S	D	■	■	■
■	■	■	L	E	K	■	D	O	L	E
S	A	F	A	R	I	■	I	D	E	A
O	N	L	I	N	E	■	N	O	G	S
S	T	Y	L	E	S	■	G	R	O	T

62

S	T	A	P	H	■	F	L	E	S	H
R	I	L	E	Y	■	L	E	N	T	O
I	M	P	R	E	C	A	T	I	O	N
■	■	■	K	N	O	T	■	D	A	K
A	C	T	■	A	R	T	S	■	■	■
I	R	I	S	■	T	E	L	U	G	U
D	E	N	O	M	I	N	A	T	O	R
S	W	E	A	R	S	■	B	A	R	N
■	■	■	P	R	O	S	■	H	E	S
G	A	T	■	I	N	C	H	■	■	■
E	X	A	G	G	E	R	A	T	E	D
M	O	R	P	H	■	U	V	U	L	A
S	N	O	O	T	■	B	E	N	D	Y

63

O	A	T	S	■	G	A	G	G	E	D
B	L	O	T	■	A	G	O	U	T	I
I	O	W	A	■	N	U	A	N	C	E
S	E	N	T	I	N	E	L	■	■	■
■	■	S	U	R	E	■	I	S	I	S
O	F	F	S	E	T	■	E	C	R	U
B	I	O	■	■	■	■	R	O	D	■
E	L	L	S	■	P	A	T	E	N	S
Y	O	K	E	■	A	N	E	W	■	■
■	■	■	E	N	V	I	A	B	L	E
F	O	S	S	A	E	■	B	A	A	L
A	U	P	A	I	R	■	A	L	M	S
T	R	A	W	L	S	■	G	L	E	E

64

■	O	D	D	S	■	H	A	S	P	■
P	R	I	A	M	■	A	G	A	R	S
A	I	S	L	E	■	N	O	N	E	T
C	O	P	■	L	S	D	■	F	L	U
E	L	A	S	T	I	C	■	R	I	P
R	E	S	T	■	M	A	D	A	M	E
■	■	S	A	D	I	R	O	N	■	■
S	P	I	R	A	L	■	E	C	R	U
T	A	O	■	P	A	L	S	I	E	S
O	W	N	■	P	R	O	■	S	H	E
M	I	A	U	L	■	O	C	C	U	R
A	N	T	R	E	■	K	O	A	N	S
■	G	E	N	S	■	S	O	N	G	■

SOLUTIONS

65

C	B	S		P	E	A		
H	O	W		L	O	G		S	E	E
A	N	E	M	O	N	E		P	A	P
I	N	E	R	T		S	C	A	R	E
N	I	T	S			A	C	N	E
S	E	T		A	C	T	R	E	S	S
	A	F	F	A	I	R	S	
P	A	L	E	T	T	E		T	A	B
L	I	K	E			N	A	G	A
A	M	I	S	S		M	O	T	E	L
T	E	N		I	M	A	G	I	N	E
E	R	G		T	E	C		O	D	E
		E	W	E		N	A	N

66

P	I	C	A	S		G	L	I	B
H	O	B	N	O	B		M	E	N	U
I	N	S	I	N	U	A	T	I	N	G
	M	A	R	C
A	S	T	E	R		I	S	N	T
C	H	I		O	D	I	O	U	S
H	E	A	R	T	H	S	T	O	N	E
E	R	R	O	R	S		K	E	G
	D	A	T	A		B	A	S	S	O
	P	E	E	L
B	E	S	T	S	E	L	L	E	R	S
A	R	I	A		C	O	A	T	E	E
D	A	R	N		W	Y	A	T	T

67

A	T	C	O		O	T	T	E	R
M	P	A	A		J	O	R	G	E
P	S	S	T		D	O	S	A	G	E
	T	H	A	I		I	F	S
U	P	A		S	M	U	R	F
N	A	N		H	E	N		I	N	A
L	Y	E		I	S	E		C	O	M
V	E	Y		E	T	A		C	P	I
	E	U	R	O	S		I	E	D
L	O	N		R	E	A	R
B	O	V	I	N	E		I	C	O	N
A	C	E	O	F		L	L	D	S
T	A	R	N	S		S	E	E	A

68

M	A	D	A	M		S	C	A	L	D
I	T	A	L	Y		C	O	R	E	R
S	T	R	A	N	G	U	L	A	T	E
S	U	N		A	L	L		C	H	A
A	N	I		S	O	L		H	A	M
L	E	N	S		M	E	A	N	L	Y
	G	A	L		R	H	O
L	U	N	G	E	S		A	P	S	E
A	P	E		A	L	B		H	E	N
I	K	E		G	O	O		O	A	T
R	E	D	O	U	B	T	A	B	L	E
D	E	L	V	E		C	R	I	E	R
S	P	E	A	R		H	E	A	D	S

69

D	U	F	F		S	F	C	S
O	S	R	I	C		H	A	O	L	E
L	A	U	G	H		A	N	N	U	L
O	U	I		I	S	R		C	D	R
O	S	T		T	A	P		E	G	O
P	A	Y	S		Y	E	N	N	E	D
	P	I	A	N	I	S	T
K	L	E	P	T	O		C	R	A	B
C	A	B		A	T	C		A	P	O
A	M	B		L	O	L		T	I	L
R	O	L	L	O		A	M	I	C	I
S	U	E	T	S		W	O	O	E	D
	R	S	S	S		E	N	S	E

70

B	O	I	S	E		B	U	F	F
E	N	N	E	A		L	A	I	L	A
C	A	D	E	T		E	L	L	A	S
O	D	E		M	A	S		E	R	A
M	A	T		E	L	S		E	E	N
E	R	E	I		G	E	N	X
S	E	R	G	E		D	E	T	A	T
	M	A	A	M		T	E	S	H
A	M	I		S	A	S		N	S	A
R	A	N		T	O	P		S	A	N
A	R	A	C	E		I	N	I	N	K
M	I	T	E	R		E	M	O	T	E
N	E	O	N		L	I	N	E	D

71

	P	R	O	S		I	N	C	A	S
A	L	A	R	M		M	O	O	R	E
D	E	S	T	I	N	A	T	I	O	N
D	U	P		T	E	G		N	U	S
E	R	E		T	W	O		E	N	E
D	A	D	O	E	S		O	D	D	S
	I	N	P	U	T
B	U	R	L		A	N	T	I	C	S
E	R	A		U	P	S		M	O	P
D	A	T		N	E	T		P	S	I
I	N	T	E	R	R	O	G	A	T	E
M	I	A	M	I		P	A	L	E	D
S	A	T	U	P		S	L	E	D

72

M	O	P		F	E	W		M	A	L
I	D	A		A	N	I		A	L	Y
C	O	N	T	R	A	C	T	I	O	N
	C	H	I	C	K	A	D	E	E
S	P	R	I	N	T	E	R
A	R	E	N	A		D	A	R	L	A
R	E	A			E	A	N
A	S	S	T	D		L	A	V	I	E
	E	U	G	E	N	I	C	S
E	M	B	A	R	R	A	S	S
B	I	L	L	I	O	N	A	I	R	E
A	T	V		N	U	T		O	A	R
N	E	D		G	T	O		N	I	A

SOLUTIONS

73

```
G E E █ M A N █ V F W
T I M P A N I █ E R O
I S S U I N G █ L E V
█ █ █ G L E E █ A Y E
A L A S S █ R E R A N
D A E █ █ E I N █ █ █
J A C T I T A T I O N
█ S C H █ █ █ G M C █
P I Q U E █ D I N A R
O S U █ D U R A █ █ █
R E I █ T R A G E D Y
E E E █ E N F O R C E
S A T █ A S T █ B C S
```

74

```
A S C A P █ R U B O N
S T O L E █ O T A R U
E A R E D █ S T R A T
A N D R E W W E I L █
█ H O O S I E R █ █ █
N O V █ █ I L L U M E
S P A T S █ L Y S O L
C E N S O R █ S R O █
█ E V E N B E T █ █ █
C A L I F O R N I A █
E E N I E █ M I A M I
S C O O T █ A N T E D
C A S T S █ D E E R E
```

75

```
R U B E █ N E A T E R
A P R S █ O N S I D E
R I A A █ N T E S T S
A N G U L A R █ █ █ █
█ █ █ E M E R I T I █
C A N I N E █ O S H A
A R E C A █ I B S E N
V I V E █ E L B O W S
A P E L I K E █ █ █ █
█ █ █ O B T R U D E █
D E B O N E █ Y S E R
S E A A I R █ A D A S
M O N T A G █ S A N T
```

76

```
M A N O S █ S T A I N
A D A G E █ H E N C E
W O R L D B E A T E R
█ █ R E A L █ R E D O
S P A █ N E E D █ █ █
L U T E █ W E R E N T
A M O N G █ C O M E R
P A R S E S █ P I C A
█ H E L P █ S K Y █ █
A F A R █ I R I S █ █
S A G I T T A R I U S
I N A N E █ N O O S E
A G R E E █ A N N E X
```

77

```
S E A G A L █ C E O
I N F E S T █ B O X Y
T A R T A R S A U C E
S C A T S █ O I L E R
A T M O █ S P R E E S
T S E █ S T O N E D █
█ █ B E E R S █ █ █ █
█ S M I L E S █ G S A
B E A K E R █ A R A N
A D M E N █ B R A N D
C U B R E P O R T E R
O C A S █ C H A I S E
N E S █ T R Y S T S
```

78

```
C A W E D █ D A D E
O P E R E █ E L E C
R O B I N L E A C H
P C B █ N A D I R
█ █ B E G S █ E C U
C L O T H O █ S A A B
H A N E Y █ S U S H I
I T O N █ F A G E N D
T E N █ I L R E
█ █ D E T O O █ A A M
T A B E R N A C L E
A G A R █ G R I M E
B A N S █ S A D A T
```

79

```
A L L A █ H O B N O B
M O E T █ I N L O V E
B L V D █ G E T M A D
I L I A █ H A S S L E
█ █ T W O P M █ █ █ █
P L A N A R █ I R K
T O T █ T E Y █ M O A
A C E █ S E A N C E
█ █ A S O L O █ █ █ █
O R M O L U █ O T O S
D I E T E R █ N Y N Y
E C A R T E █ Z O O S
R E L O A D █ O U S T
```

80

```
A S I T I S █ U N I V
S T R A T A █ G O N E
C A R E S S █ A N T I
E Y E █ O H I █ C A L
N E C █ K A R A O K E
T R O T █ Y E N N E D
█ V O N █ D E F █ █ █
C L E R I C █ T O S S
O A R S M A N █ R E A
S S A █ S U E █ M A W
I S B N █ S A H I B S
G I L A █ E L Y S E E
N E E T █ S E P T E T
```

SOLUTIONS

81

```
BASS  ADSORB
ALUM  BEARER
ROSEKENNEDY
REPRO  TEGAN
  ESSAYS
SINH  ANTCOW
ELD  ENE  OCA
RASHAD  MATS
   ATEOUT
CCLVI  ASTRA
HELENOFTROY
ODDITY  NEVE
PISTOL  TEES
```

82

```
GUPTA  TBILL
ATREE  OLLIE
SEERS  MOIRA
  TRON  OARS
JOE  POND
ELEE  VERNAL
SINCE  PEONS
UNSAID  DANA
  UNCO  HOT
TVAD  LTDS
EILAT  ORARE
TILTS  EARTH
RISER  SYKES
```

83

```
CHAFF  EATIT
LONER  ARENA
ELIDE  MINCE
FALSETEETH
    ZEST
MEAGER  TEDS
ALTAR  CADET
BIOS  DASHER
   ONUS
 COLORATURA
BAKES  BANAL
ELENI  AKIRA
EIDER  SATAN
```

84

```
MACED  TRUES
EPODE  HOMME
DEMOB  RABID
UMP  ADORING
SEATTLE  LEE
ANNIES  NIMS
  INS  ROC
BBOY  DETAIL
IAN  LAJOLLA
ARAPAHO  CDS
FIBER  INOUT
RULED  CIRCE
AMESS  ENDED
```

85

```
SUM  ALF
CPI  RAE  OTC
ORS  USEDCAR
TOTEM  SEEME
TARR  SALE
OREGANO  NAP
  ASFARAS
GAT  REDRESS
ARMA  ILEA
SLEDS  ALERT
PENDANT  VER
EST  AIT  ENA
  RMS  NEP
```

86

```
SARIS  STAGS
NTEST  HELOT
ORDIE  RETAR
PIUS  PESETA
ESC  LAD  REI
SKEWER  ANET
  TOSTADA
OMOO  TOMTOM
LOT  AWL  IMO
ENESCO  AVER
AGAIN  ABELE
TORRE  ARLES
ELSES  SAYTO
```

87

```
CGI  ASS  IDS
ANC  LOY  NUT
PUEBLOS  UKE
  LITTORAL
LIVEN  OBESE
ALAS  OLD
HORSDOEUVRE
  YAH  REAM
ENVOY  OATHS
MONUMENT
PRE  ARSENIC
TIC  ROE  ONE
YAK  EST  GNP
```

88

```
MOLL  FIFA
AREAS  MINES
NITTI  GATTO
NOTED  ONHER
ILEX  CEST
XER  ELSES
 SCRAPHEAP
AETNA  MAH
SSRS  MELO
ATREE  HAVEA
RAINS  SMEAR
TIETO  NAILS
ORRS  SNEE
```

SOLUTIONS

89

```
S A S S Y   M A G M A
E M C E E   A L I A S
G I A N T   M O N T H
O D D S   D A N
      O B I   G O O S
S W I R L E D   A B A
H A D   A T E   T O N
I R E   B A N S H E E
P E A T   R Y E
      H A Y   A L S O
L A P E L   D A Y A N
I N U R E   D I R G E
T Y P E S   T R E S S
```

90

```
M I N   B P S   E W W
A G O   R E E   M H O
C O R P O R A T I O N
H O M E     T I R E D
I N S E C T   C A V E
    R A I L   T E R
  M A Y F L O W E R
T A M   E D D O
A L O P   E E R I E R
T A R O T     T R U E
T R O P O S P H E R E
L I U   A L A   N O S
E A S   D A Y   E S E
```

91

```
B O L U S   A H A B
U N A R Y   S E L E S
R E M O N S T R A T E
L E E   O O O   R R S
A Y S   D L R   M A E
P E A R   D I T S Y
    U M I A K
  S E T A E   O L E N
B U N   D R Y   I N O
L T S   D O E   E G O
O R I G I N A L S I N
W A G O N   R E I N E
  S N A G   N I N E S
```

92

```
A V O W S   A N D E S
S E R A L   R A R E E
H E N R Y   I R E N A
C R A N E   E R W I N
A I M S     A B E S
N E E   E V I T A
  S N I V E L E R S
  T N O T E   R E M
S T A T     P Y R O
O A T E N   L I M E S
A L I N E   E T O N S
M O O S E   T H R E E
I N N E D   A Y E R S
```

93

```
S I R E N   A R I A L
I S A Y A   T E E N A
C I N E S   A M A S S
S T A L A C T I T E
    F I L L I N
L I T D   O L D P R O
O B E   C S T   A D A
M O R E A U   S R A S
    I R R U P T
  G O D F E A R I N G
M A D E A   N A T A L
O M A R R   D I A N A
P A S S E   I N S U M
```

94

```
S H U T S   O O H S
T O N Y A   O B E Y S
P U R P L E H E A R T
E D E   S N L   N I E
T O S T A D A   E A R
E N T R   E L A Y N E
    I S A A C
A S I M O V   M O S H
R P M   R O B E R T A
U R E   T R L   M E R
M I L L I S E C O N D
S E D A N   E R R O L
  R A N G   P O E S Y
```

95

```
B B L S   O P P S
O O O L A   S L A T E
I V O R Y   M O R A N
L I S   A P O   A T O
E N E   H O S   P U L
R E A D   R I C H E S
  S U I T S M E
S C A R N E   D R N O
C O G   A N C   N O D
O R O   M T A   A V I
W R O T E   P Y L E S
L A S E S   S A I N T
  L E E S   M A A S
```

96

```
S T O M P   B A S H
T A N I A   S A S H A
P R E D E C E S S O R
A G O   S O A   U W E
T E N   E N G   R E M
S T E M   S O M E R S
    A B C D E
C U R S O R   D A L E
O R O   O I L   B E A
S S S   T P S   S A S
T I C K E T A G E N T
A N O L E   T E N T O
S E E M   S E T O N
```

SOLUTIONS

97

	B	E	R	T	H	S			
R	A	N	A	W	A	Y		C	A	F
A	R	T	W	O	R	K		A	B	A
E	N	E			K	E	R	N	E	L
S	E	R	V	E		S	I	D	E	S
	S	T	E	L	A		P	Y	R	E
	A	R	I	S	T	O	S			
E	R	I	S		S	O	F	T	C	
L	I	N	E	R		A	F	R	E	E
A	C	I	D	I	C		I	L	E	
T	A	N		N	O	H	O	P	E	R
E	N	G		S	O	R	C	E	R	Y
		O	L	E	A	R	Y			

98

M	U	D	S			A	R	L	O	S
I	L	E	A		I	M	E	L	D	A
S	E	A	U		N	O	T	B	A	D
C	E	L	T	I	C		U	S	S	R
		M	E	D	I	A	N			
G	B	E		I	N	F	E	R	N	O
M	R	I		O	E	R		E	A	N
S	I	N	A	T	R	A		C	B	S
		I	S	A	I	A	H			
A	S	T	R		T	D	B	A	N	K
W	E	E	P	I	E		E	R	G	O
A	G	E	O	L	D		A	G	O	N
D	A	M	P	S			M	E	S	A

99

S	C	I	S	S	O	R		S	S	A
C	A	S	C	A	D	E		T	O	T
H	P	L	O	V	E	C	R	A	F	T
E	L	A	T	E	D		I	N	T	I
M	E	N	S			A	S	N	E	R
E	T	D		T	A	K	E	O	N	E
		K	E	F	I	R				
V	I	T	A	M	I	N		R	O	M
I	C	E	U	P			D	E	N	Y
R	O	A	R		B	E	E	P	A	T
I	N	S	I	D	E	S	T	O	R	Y
L	I	E		T	A	P	E	S	U	P
E	C	T		S	T	Y	R	E	N	E

100

C	O	P	E	D		A	D	E	P	T
O	V	O	L	O		R	E	V	U	E
S	A	L	V	E		T	E	E	N	S
	L	I	S	P		P	S	S	T	
E	G	I	S		H	I	S			
L	O	W		S	I	D	E	A	R	M
U	B	O	A	T		L	A	N	A	I
L	I	G	N	I	T	E		T	I	N
		I	R	A		R	E	N	D	
C	E	S	S		U	R	E	A		
A	S	K	E	W		A	T	T	A	R
P	A	Y	E	E		S	I	E	G	E
S	U	E	D	E		H	E	R	O	D

101

A	M	E	S			F	I	T	I	N
N	C	A	A			A	N	I	T	A
T	A	R	S		G	E	R	M	A	N
		T	S	A	R		E	E	L	
A	S	H		M	A	M	M	A		
H	O	C		E	P	A		N	S	A
E	R	E		L	E	N		D	T	S
M	E	N		I	N	A		M	A	E
		T	H	E	U	N		O	R	A
E	E	E		T	A	C	T			
S	T	R	E	S	S		O	I	S	E
O	N	E	L	S			C	O	A	L
H	A	D	S	T			O	N	E	S

102

	A	L	O	H	A		E	T	A	
R	O	G	E	T			Y	O	U	
P	O	L	A	R	B	E	A	R		
	S	E	R	I	A	L				
H	O	E	S			S	E	G	A	R
A	S	L		A	U	S	T	E	R	E
W	H	I	S	T	L	E	S	T	O	P
K	E	P	T	O	U	T		W	O	O
E	A	S	E	D			A	I	M	S
		E	D	G	A	R	S			
P	E	R	S	O	N	N	E	L		
A	C	E		A	K	I	T	A		
S	O	D		T	H	E	O	C		

103

I	M	I	N	E		B	R	O	S
T	A	N	E	Y		L	E	O	V	I
A	S	F	A	R		E	L	L	E	N
S	K	I	L	I	F	T		L	R	G
C	E	N		E	L	S		O	D	E
A	D	I	O		O	U	T	F	O	R
		T	E	N	S	P	O	T		
O	P	E	R	A	S		A	H	A	S
D	A	S		S	I	G		E	M	I
O	R	I		D	E	R	I	D	E	D
N	E	M	E	A		A	G	I	R	L
T	R	A	N	Q		B	O	C	C	E
O	S	L	O			S	T	E	E	R

104

B	M	W	S			S	B	A	R	R	O
L	E	H	R			W	O	N	O	U	T
I	R	A	S			O	R	G	A	N	O
P	C	T		H	O	I		R	A	E	
	I	O	N	E	S	C	O				
O	F	F	I	S	H		B	A	S	S	
R	U	I	N	S			R	E	L	O	S
A	L	T	O		W	A	S	A	B	I	
		N	E	A	T	E	N	S			
I	E	D		S	K	A		A	T	L	
S	T	E	P	P	E		A	L	O	E	
A	R	E	Y	O	U		B	D	R	M	
W	E	T	M	O	P		C	A	Y	S	

SOLUTIONS

105

```
M A M I E . T A M E .
A D O R N . A L O N G
R E B A G . L A D L E
D L I . A B O . E I N
I A L . R E S O L V E
. E R D E . T I E R .
A L A T E . S E N N A
P A L E . B E A T . .
I N A S P I N . E S O
C O B . A C E . R E M
A L A S S . C H I N A
L I M I T . A R O A R
. N A L A . S E R T A
```

106

```
T A P E R . A L I A S
A U R A E . B E N N E
E D I T S . B A S I C
L I S . I C E . I L O
S O M E D A Y . P I N
. . D U P . H I N D .
F R E E T R A D E . .
M U O N . I O U . . .
O C A . O V U L A T E
P H D . K E N . N I M
E S T E R . D H O L E
D I A N A . E I D E R
S A X E S . D E E D Y
```

107

```
B A N . S O N . A D D
W R Y . T W O . L E I
A R M O R E D C A R S
N A P P E S . A M I S
A S H E N . C L O V E
. . . D U P E . D E C
A B A . O A R . E S T
T E L . U S E R . . .
T A L E S . B O F F S
A R Y L . A R T E R Y
C H I L L F A C T O R
H U N . E A T . U Z I
E G G . A R E . S E A
```

108

```
R O A M O F F . F L A
E L L A M A E . E O S
N E W Y E A R S D A Y
A S E A N . R I O D E
M O S S . G A R R E T
E N T . R E R E A D .
. . A E R I E . . . .
. S P A S M S . R E F
P H E L P S . S E S E
R A N T O . H O I S E
U N C O N C E R N E D
D I I . S I S T I N E
E A L . E D A S N E R
```

109

```
A W L S . I S M E . .
M O O G . S H A R D .
B O O T . S I E N N A
E D S . I A T . I I N
R E E . C S I . F E E
S N A K E S . H E S S
. . S E S A M E S . .
B E A N . F O R T I S
R A G . O R A . A R E
I G O . G A T . T O R
E L O P E S . C I N E
R E S E E . C O O N .
. S E C S . I N N E .
```

110

```
. A G H A . P A N S Y
P L I E D . A G A P E
H E M A L . S E T I N
D E P R E S S I O N .
. . . T R E K S . . .
A L P S . A E T H E R
R E V . P L Y . A K A
P I C A R O . A M E N
. . . G O F O R . . .
. D I R T F A R M E R
D O N E E . R O O M Y
D U K E S . E Y R I E
T R Y S T . D O E R .
```

111

```
M I L . N S A . A S H
C R I . B L T . D E A
C A L M W E A T H E R
V E A U . E X E D R A
. . . S A T Y R . . .
I B I S E S . Z B A R
T I M O R . I A M S O
A P P L . U N R I P E
. . . I S S E I . . .
S H A N I A . M G R S
M O W I N G L A W N S
O Y L . K E Y . A A R
G A S . S S S . R S S
```

112

```
H O M E . T E M P T
A C I D Y . O D O R S
I T S M E . R E S O W
L A T . T H E . Q U A
T V S . I E R . U S N
O O O H . L O L I T A
. F I L M S E T . . .
O P A Q U E . M O H S
G U V . G T I . C E L
A R A . G S O . O N E
U S L T A . T R A L A
G E O R G . A S S E Z
E R N I E . S T Y E .
```

SOLUTIONS

113

E	C	O	L	I		M	A	P	L	E
R	U	N	A	T		E	D	I	C	T
D	E	C	K	O	F	C	A	R	D	S
A	D	E	E		A	C	H			
			E	T	N	A		D	S	S
P	O	I	R	O	T		S	E	E	A
P	A	N	I	C	A	T	T	A	C	K
S	H	O	E		S	H	A	F	T	S
S	U	R		I	T	E	M			
			I	N	I		P	I	P	S
S	P	A	R	E	C	H	A	N	G	E
U	S	A	I	R		S	C	R	A	M
N	T	E	S	T		I	T	I	S	I

114

C	A	P	E		O	U	S	T	E	D
T	H	E	E		C	R	E	E	P	Y
R	E	P	E	A	T	A	G	A	I	N
L	A	S		K	E	L		R	C	A
S	P	I	R	I	T	S		G	U	S
		A	S	S		D	A	R	T	
T	B	S	P	S		C	A	S	E	Y
W	A	T	T		P	A	L			
O	D	O		F	I	R	E	S	A	T
F	I	N		L	S	T		N	L	E
E	D	I	F	I	C	A	T	I	O	N
R	E	L	A	T	E		C	P	A	S
S	A	Y	Y	E	S		B	E	N	E

115

E	S	S		F	A	D				
R	E	A		A	B	A		S	R	S
R	A	N	R	I	O	T		T	H	E
A	E	S	I	R		E	F	R	O	N
T	E	E	M			L	I	N	D	
A	L	B		N	O	N	U	K	E	S
		A	S	C	R	I	B	E		
N	O	S	E	O	U	T		I	S	E
E	N	T	S			E	T	T	A	
U	R	I	E	L		C	O	R	E	S
R	Y	A		E	L	U	S	I	V	E
O	E	N		M	E	S		C	I	I
			A	U	S		H	E	N	

116

B	A	R	B	A	R	A		E	M	U
U	N	O	I	L	E	D		R	E	S
G	I	B	B	O	N	S		T	A	P
		L	E	A			E	N	S	
E	L	B	E		M	I	D	S	T	
D	A	U	B		E	R	E			
O	C	T	E	T		K	A	P	P	A
	L	E	U		T	R	A	P		
	F	A	T	A	L		H	O	L	E
C	A	D			T	A	R			
H	U	M		M	I	N	A	R	E	T
A	N	A		E	M	O	T	I	V	E
P	A	N		G	O	N	E	B	A	D

117

S	A	M	B	A		S	P	O	T	S
O	R	A	L	S		M	I	N	E	O
W	O	R	T	S		O	N	E	A	L
H	U	T		N	O	T		I	S	A
A	S	H		S	C	H		N	E	C
T	E	A	M		D	E	B	A	T	E
		S	A	C		R	A	M		
A	C	T	I	O	N		H	I	N	D
D	O	E		A	L	E		L	E	A
D	O	W		R	E	D		L	T	S
S	T	A	T	S		S	M	I	T	H
T	E	R	S	E		E	C	O	L	E
O	R	T	O	N		L	I	N	E	D

118

C	L	E	F	S		B	I	B	L	E
H	I	N	D	U		U	S	H	E	R
I	N	C	A	R	C	E	R	A	T	E
R	E	A		E	A	N		K	O	S
A	A	S		B	S	O		T	U	T
C	L	E	V	E	S		S	I	T	U
		S	T	E	T	S				
L	O	L	O		R	O	A	M	E	D
A	R	I		E	O	E		A	R	E
T	S	O		T	L	C		N	N	E
K	I	N	D	H	E	A	R	T	E	D
E	N	E	R	O		P	A	R	S	E
S	O	L	E	S		S	L	A	T	E

119

S	A	D	H	U		L	A	B	O	R
C	R	E	E	S		A	P	A	C	E
A	C	C	R	A		C	E	R	T	S
L	A	O		G	N	U		G	A	T
A	N	N		E	O	N		A	V	E
R	A	T	A		M	A	Z	I	E	R
		A	R	T	I	S	A	N		
S	U	M	M	O	N		P	H	A	T
A	N	I		R	E	S		U	R	I
U	R	N		R	E	T		N	I	P
C	E	A	S	E		E	S	T	O	P
E	A	T	E	N		T	H	E	S	E
S	L	E	E	T		S	H	R	E	D

120

M	A	P	L	E		A	R	T	U	R
I	T	R	A	N		S	H	O	N	E
R	H	I	N	O		T	E	R	R	I
I	O	N	A		P	R	O	T	O	N
A	M	C		G	R	O		O	L	A
M	E	E	T	M	E		O	I	L	S
		V	I	C	T	I	M	S		
A	V	A	S		E	M	B	E	D	S
G	I	L		H	E	A		S	E	L
E	D	I	S	O	N		O	H	S	O
N	E	A	R	S		A	D	E	E	P
C	O	N	T	E		M	E	L	E	E
Y	S	T	A	D		B	A	L	D	S

SOLUTIONS

121

```
CAP   MAO   NOD
AGA   IMP   ORE
TRINKET   TIC
TESTER   SEGO
YEAH   ITALIC
      COGENT
 CASTANETS
LOCKIN
AROUND   ADDS
ZOLA   REDRAW
ANY   SESSILE
RAT   AAA   ELD
SEE   EMU   DYE
```

122

```
INST   MASSED
DATE   ILLUSE
ETAL   TWENTY
SOREHEAD
   SCARY   MAP
ALIAS   SMALL
CIGS   AGUE
MONTH   PRIMA
ENS   OPTIC
    JALAPENO
CESURA   OYER
HOUNDS   SEAT
INMESH   ASPS
```

123

```
PAPA   MADCAP
EGOS   AREOLA
RAWS   SALMAN
URDU   TNT
  ERNE   ABED
CAREER   SERE
ARK   TSP   TON
LIED   ARREST
MAGI   TOON
   ERA   LOAD
CAUSER   LIKE
INSEAM   ERIE
STALLS   REND
```

124

```
ALT   FRA
NEA   REN   TSO
NEP   EYEWEAR
ARETE   SINGA
LARS   INAN
STEPINS   INT
  CSLEWIS
EVO   SOFARAS
NORW   GALE
TIDAL   TOCKS
ELEVATE   KAA
RAR   DAS   ELM
   ABS   TIE
```

125

```
ALAS   DEIST
CIAOS   ISNEW
EERIE   ASSAI
ISO   ECG   IER
ITN   ARR   DEL
COSA   EASELS
   PLUMMET
MTETNA   IHOP
AOL   ATC   ECO
DOL   WEE   PTL
AKITA   IZAAK
SONAR   LORNA
ANGIE   EKES
```

126

```
WHARF   REEVE
EULER   ORIEL
AGAMA   BORED
RECONSIDER
   ARCANE
AGRA   RIDDEN
TNT   FDA   ERE
MUESLI   STAB
   TANNER
 BURGEONING
MONAD   RETIE
OSTIA   SCULL
PHONY   EASES
```

127

```
BASRA   CASAS
ONHER   OBAMA
TOOLE   NOTIN
HAVANACUBA
  ETAPE
UGLI   IDIOCY
NUEVE   ENNIS
ENDEAR   CEIL
  SERIO
 PHOEBESNOW
BUENO   AIOLI
MTWTF   DONAT
WASOF   ANENT
```

128

```
PEDAL   GRASS
AKINS   TOSEE
DEANA   SANKA
  METS   DOOM
ERES   LEB
SAT   URGESON
ONEPM   ADELE
STRAPON   LAA
   PSP   CANT
PLIE   ACES
EAVES   ASSAY
RIATA   RAISE
ERNES   AREST
```

SOLUTIONS

129

```
S M U G _ _ S M I T E
H A N A _ _ T A M I L
A N D Y _ G R I P E D
D I E _ E R E _ E T E
E A R _ V O W _ R A S
S C E N I C _ A C C T
_ _ S T E E L I E _ _
M O T H _ R U M P U S
A R I _ E I K _ T N T
T I M _ N E E _ I S A
H E A R T S _ A B A T
I N T E R _ A L F A _
S T E V E _ R E E L _
```

130

```
C H E E K _ P E S C I
H O Y L E _ A S H E N
G R E A S Y S P O O N
_ _ G L E E _ R O S E
M I L _ Y A L E _ _ _
A S A S _ H I S S A T
R A S P S _ E S T A S
G O S L O W _ O T R O
_ _ O H H I _ H E S _
I M I T _ E N T O _ _
B E N C H W A R M E R
E I G H T _ G I A D A
T R E Y S _ E P S O N
```

131

```
A R C H A I C _ _ _ _
L O R E T T A _ H C H
A B Y S M A L _ A R A
N O S H _ N E R V E S
O T T E R _ I E S T _
N S A _ E S S E N C E
_ L E F T O U T _ _ _
S U B S I D Y _ A C H
I S A O _ S O C L E _
M U L L A H _ F L A M
O R L _ N U R T U R E
N Y S _ A G R E E O N
_ _ _ S O S A _ _ _ _
```

132

```
A B E D _ _ A S C O T
P A L E _ _ M E L B A
T H E N _ U P R O O T
_ _ C Y A N _ U S E _
G O T _ S H A M E _ _
E R R _ S A P _ D A B
L E I _ U R I _ C O O
D O C _ R N A _ I N N
_ _ C H E E R _ R E D
_ T H O _ S Y N C _ _
H E A R T S _ O U S T
A M I D E _ D I E S _
S P R E E _ S T E P _
```

133

```
I N S P _ _ O N C D S
T O O T H _ A G A M E
I N P U T _ T O R A S
_ _ H I T E M _ P J S
R A I _ P L E B E _ _
S P E C _ F A T T E D
S I S I S _ L U C I E
S A C R E D _ S L R S
_ _ H O C U S _ E E K
O B O _ E B O L A _ _
T R I A D _ U A N D I
T Y C H E _ P T E R O
O N E A D _ S R I S _
```

134

```
E E L _ T A B _ P T A
M O A _ O C A _ Y O N
U N C L U T T E R E D
_ _ _ A R I O S O _ _
M A I D E N N A M E S
O W N E R _ S U A V E
T A D _ _ _ N E D _ _
O R I E L _ S U I N G
R E C R I M I N A T E
_ _ A N N U L I _ _ _
P E N E T R A T I O N
A R T _ E R G _ M B A
W A S _ L E E _ P I G
```

135

```
O R B S _ K N E E S _
R O U E _ N U T M E G
A B R A C A D A B R A
T I P _ E V E _ A I M
E N S U R E _ R O E _
_ _ R E S T _ G U T _
S A U N A _ A R O S E
A N N _ L O T H _ _ _
L O S _ S T O L I D _
S I N _ G P O _ O N E
A N A C H R O N I S M
S T R I A E _ O R E O
_ S L A T Y _ W E T S
```

136

```
C A D _ A I D _ _ _ _
O R I _ C S I _ R U M
A L S _ C H O L E R A
T E A R S _ N O C A N
I N G A _ _ A O N E _
S E R P E N T _ L O T
_ E T H I C A L _ _ _
T I E _ S N I P E A T
O N M E _ _ A C M E _
S T E A M _ O T T E R
C E N T A V O _ I N C
A L T _ L I Z _ O R E
_ A R E _ N A L _ _ _
```

SOLUTIONS

137

```
S A K E S   L A V A S
I R E N A   A T I L T
S E E D Y   S E R T A
T O P   S O C   G A B
E L I   T U A   I R S
R A T A   T R A N
S E A L S   S C R I P
    S L U E   R E L O
A A E   C C S   C O M
U F C   C G I   O V A
N O R S E   C E R E D
T R E A S   E D D I E
S E T T S   M A S T S
```

138

```
O F F S   I C I C L E
S I L T   B E M O A N
T R O I   I A M B I C
E S P R E S S O
R T E   L E E R S A T
  R A C K S   T I T O
L A R A S   C A N T O
U T E P   G U L C H
S E D A R I S   E E E
    C A R P A R T S
R E M I N D   B E I T
P U T T E E   A L M A
G R A Y E R   T Y E S
```

139

```
A L I C E S   T H A I
F A N O U T   S O P S
B A N G L E   K E P T
  U S E   C T R L S
C O E   R N A S
O L N   U N K N O T
L L D   M R I   A C T
T A O I S M   M H O
    B R I M   E S P
B L E E P   I F S
O R C A   P A L A T E
L O O M   H O O K U P
A N N S   D W E E B S
```

140

```
S T A T U E   S A G A
A S M A R A   P C B S
N A O M I S   O A S T
D R O P   Y A R D
      O C T E T
F O R M   N E I M A N
B R E A K T H E I C E
S E A R C H   R A S A
  M C R A E
    T I R E   B A B S
L E I A   Y O O H O O
A L O G   E N R O L L
P O N E   S T A P L E
```

141

```
H U L U   A L C A P P
I N A S   R E U S E S
R A Y B R A D B U R Y
E P T   I M O   N F C
S T O O D I N   D U H
    M E S   H E M E
T A P E S   C A R E D
A L A N   S E I
R I N   D U N G E O N
B E A   A C S   S N O
U N C O N C E R N E D
S E E N T O   P E A U
H E A T E R   I S L S
```

142

```
S E C T   P O S E R
A C H E   D A R K L Y
S H A H   A E D I L E
H O R R I B L E
    L A C   L A N C E
C R A N E   A L E R T
L I T   F A A
A G A R S   S T A B S
M A N I A   A I R
    S U R P R I S E
P E T I T E   A O N E
A T O N E D   D U A L
D A N G S   E S P Y
```

143

```
P A S T I S   C A P
A C C E D E   A G A
S T R E E T C R E D
S O A N D S O S
E R M A   I M A M A N
    A N I L I N E
S H A L L   N E C C O
T O T E B A G
S O F T E N   P A C E
    S I N G U L A R
M A R T I A L A R T
A M I   E N S I L E
S A P   S T E N O S
```

144

```
C R I B S   L E A K
B A R R E   A D D L E
S T R I P   V I V I D
    E M I T   T E N D
I M P   A I M   N E O
R O L L   S O F T
A W A I T   A D U L T
    C E R T   A R E A
T E E   Y O U   E A T
A L A R   O N U S
T I B I A   C L O S E
A T L A S   U N M A N
  E E L S   T A E L S
```

SOLUTIONS

145

```
M O P E S   S P I L L
F A I R E   M A N E D
A T T E N   A L O E S
S Y S C O   R A N T
      T R I T T
M A P S   S E E O U T
A A A   S S R   B S E
T E S T E E   S O D A
      R A I S A
  P L E B   L H A S A
A R U B A   A A R O N
L I N E S   B R A W N
L E E K S   S A L S A
```

146

```
E N B L O C     A H A
S E R A P H     N O R
T R O U P E S   G Y M
E V O   O C D   E D A
S E M I S K I L L E D
    N E O   O O N A
  P E N D U L O U S
T O N I   T A I
H O M E S T R E T C H
E R A   T I C   I R A
A B S   S M E L T E R
I O S   E N C A M P
R Y E   S Y D N E Y
```

147

```
A L L A   B O N N E T
D E E S   E R O I C A
O A T S   M A S C O T
  S I L E N T
I L L G O   T R I S
L E O N A   S A L A D
E G O       L O I
S U S I E   D R A N O
  P E N T   C A T E S
    S H R I N E
E R M I N E   C A F E
R E A D I N   I S I N
S E L E C T   D E N T
```

148

```
C E D E S   S A L E
A L O F T   P O E T
S A N T A M A R I A
T N T   R E N T
    A F T   A L S O
S P E C I E S   A H A
E A V E S   U D D E R
E R E   H A R N E S S
D A N K   R C A
    A G U E   M B A
P Y R O M A N I A C
T O M E   S O L A R
A D A R   E R O S E
```

149

```
A R E A M A P   A B A
P E R S O N A   N E S
T E N N I S S H O E S
E L I E L   T O M M Y
S E E R   A R T I E R
T D S   C H A S E R
    R O O M Y
  S O O N Y I   R O K
A T O D D S   V E R E
P A L A U   C O P S E
I R O N C U R T A I N
A V G   T S A R I N A
N E Y   S E W E D O N
```

150

```
A L A M O   P L E A D
T A C O S   S E L M A
T R A N S L A T I O N
A E C   E I N   S R A
C D I   O K D   S A S
H O A R   E Q U A L
    A B A S E
M O N O S   Y E S I
D A S   O H H   N A N
I S T   H O D   S U E
C A L L I T Q U I T S
E L E V S   R A G E S
S A R I S   S E N S E
```

151

```
A C T I N   C O R D S
L O O S E   A B O U T
L U R I D   N I O B E
O P T S   F E T T L E
W O O   H O R   B I D
S N I P E R   D E N S
    S O M E O N E
A B E D   S C A R A B
N O S   T E A   F L U
A D H E R E   G L E N
D I E G O   G O O P S
E C L A T   A G A P E
M E L D S   G O T O N
```

152

```
P R S   M C C
A E C   D R A C H M A
S S R   S U B D U E D
S E E D E D   E N S E
I D E O   O F G A B
M A N H O O D   E S T
  W A R R I O R
I S R   B U C K S A W
P O I N S   E T N A
A L T A   A N D R E I
D E E P F R Y   I M S
S A R A L E E   K I T
    O A T   E A S
```

SOLUTIONS

153

```
S O R B E T _ I C I _
T R O I K A _ I N O N _
A M U L E T _ R E N D _
R O T L _ A P I E C E _
T R E O _ I S D U E _ _
S E R F _ C S H A R P _
_ _ R A H A B _ _ _ _
G I V I N G _ R A P T _
A L I G N _ O P A H _
B O O H O O _ G A R R _
L I L T _ S T U C C O _
E L I S _ T E E H E E _
S O N _ E A S E L S _
```

154

```
D U M P S _ T A G O N
A P A R T _ A D E L E
M A R I A H C A R E Y
_ A I R E _ M E G O _
E N T _ K E N S _ _
N A H A _ P I R A C Y
G L O B E _ H I R E E
S A N S O M _ B T E N
_ E N I D _ E S S _
I S B N _ S E A R _
F O O T S O L D I E R
H O S E A _ L O A D S
E T H E L _ A G L E T
```

155

```
T I B I A _ N I K O S
V I L L E _ O R I Y A
A S A I R _ N A M E S
_ C A I N E _ K R S
E L K _ A E T N A _
N I H I L O _ O R L Y
C R A M S _ O R D I E
Y E W S _ U N N A I L
_ K O A L A _ S I P
B E D _ R A J A H _
A R O S E _ U T I C A
L E W I S _ R O A R K
L I N G O _ Y E N T A
```

156

```
D U E D A T E _ I D S
A B R A D E S _ N O T
M O R N I N G S T A R
P L A C E D _ K O L A
E T T E _ E V E N L Y
N S A _ P R O W E S S
_ C A M U S _ _ _ _
E S C A P E S _ A G R
T O O F A R _ A M I E
H U M E _ C A V E R S
I N E S T I M A B L E
C D I _ S E T S A I L
S S N _ U S S T E E L
```

157

```
A P T _ S K A T E
G R A B _ S H O W E R
H E R O _ T U R N E R
A P P O S I T E _
_ G A L _ A D O S
B E S I D E S _ I L O
O R I E L _ A G A I N
A G O _ Y U L E L O G
T O N E _ K O I _
_ P L A N G E N T
P A T O I S _ E M I R
I C I C L E _ R U N E
T E C H Y _ S E E
```

158

```
M A F I A _ A L E T A
T H I N G _ R E C O N
G A R T H _ I R O N S
_ S E A S O N _
A T T N _ U S E I T
C A R T _ C O R N E A
A C A _ O C S _ D E G
B E T I D E _ L E N O
_ T E N D S _ A L A D
_ A N S A R I _
S A O N E _ L I B R A
A B B E S _ B A L E D
R E S T S _ S T Y E S
```

159

```
S P I T _ D E B A S E
C O R E _ I N U R E S
A R R A N G E M E N T
R O U S E _ S O D A
A S P _ E M U _ L O T
B E T A _ E T H A N E
_ P I L E I _
S P A R S E _ M A G S
O I L _ M E W _ C A T
L E K S _ O U T R E
D R A W T H E L I N E
E C L A I R _ N O E L
R E I G N S _ A N T S
```

160

```
M A R S H _ G H A N A
A R E T E _ R A B I D
S O D O I _ U R A L S
I N O R D I N A T E _
_ M I N I S _
D B L S _ S O S O O N
B O O _ L P N _ C H E
A P O G E E _ M A M O
_ L A C E Y _
_ C O U N T T O T E N
T A K E I _ A P E R Y
O R L O N _ T I L D E
S L A N G _ S A L E S
```

161

```
U F O . L A D .
P A R . E V A . D A M
R E G . V E R T I G O
E R A T O . C A S E S
A I N U . . M A N E
R E I N S I N . S T Y
. Z E A L O U S .
O C A . C O N S O R T
R I T E . . E C H O
D R I L L . T R I O S
E C O L O G Y . A D S
R A N . N A P . T E E
. E Y E . E S S
```

162

```
G O T H . M E A N A
E D H S . I N M E N
N E A T . I D L E R S
I N T . R M S . L O W
A S S . E P T . I L E
L E N A P E . C O I R
. O N O R D E R .
A L T I . I D E A L S
S L R . S O A . T I T
H A I . M U Y . I B O
I N G L E S . T O R O
N O H O W . S N A G
E S T A S . E S S E
```

163

```
C A T . M T N .
O F A S O R T . W T S
S T R I D E S . A H H
T E A M . A B U S E R
A R M P I T . S T L O
. E A S E L . B E A V
R F S . R I M . D D E
A F A R . K A T E Y .
T E L E . E V E N I F
S C A L E D . G E N L
O T T . P I Z A R R O
N S A . O R A N G E S
. S T P . Y D S
```

164

```
G R I P S . S A M S A
N O F E E . A R Y A N
A S Y E T . A I S L E
R A O . R A B A T .
. U M A S S . E D M
J U D I T H . B R E A
I M O N E . L A Y E R
L P N S . K E R N E L
L S T . I N T R O .
. W I L T S . V A N
A M A T I . E N E M Y
M A N S E . A S L I P
O C T A D . T A S E D
```

165

```
H D S . A K A . G E M
O U T . L E G . I L A
H A R E B R A I N E D
O N A P A R . E G A D
S E W O N . I R E N E
. S I N N . R O N
L S T . A L T . S R S
A E R . N E E T .
S T U N S . R I M E S
A S S N . A L C A P P
G A T E C R A S H E R
N I M . D O C . R E I
A L E . E W E . E S T
```

166

```
S T U P E . W A G E
S O N O M A . S S N S
W I C K E D . W H A P
. O Y E R S . W R Y
N A N . R E N T E .
A I D E . P O O D L E
P R I M P . T E N E T
A S T A R E . D E S I
. I G O R S . S E C
E C O . B A A E D .
X E N O . O C T A D S
E B A Y . F R A Y E D
C U L L . A S S E S
```

167

```
I B O S . C R E P E S
M A L E . H E N R Y I
A R E D . A C C O R D
C I G A R S T O R E .
. K O M O D O .
L E M A N S . E G A N
A L A . . . U L U
P S T S . C H I E F S
. U N C L E S .
. T R I L O B I T E S
T I E P I N . T A D A
I N S A N E . M R I S
P O T T E D . E N T S
```